T0340372

Economic Liberalisation in Latin America

This book explores the process of economic liberalisation in Latin America and revises the transition from the import substitution industrialisation model to market-oriented reforms. It explains the theoretical foundations of the neoliberal paradigm and the implications of the policies that were labelled as the Washington Consensus. The book also incorporates an assessment on the socio-political norms added to the orthodox prescription, the so-called Post-Washington Consensus. The study comprises a general analysis on the subcontinent and on different economic liberalisation paths, and looks at four country case studies: Mexico, Brazil, Chile, and Uruguay, from the 1980s to recent years.

From this approach, the reader can analyse weaknesses and strengths, the socioeconomic performance, and the difficulties that Latin America has presented through the turbulent process of economic liberalisation, both at an early stage and over the long run, by means of country case studies encompassing the most diverse and representative styles of economic openness in the subcontinent. This allows them to identify the challenges the country faces and the appropriate policies they can follow to cope with sustained economic growth, poverty reduction, and income distribution within an economically open environment. The study is carried out by analysing and contrasting theoretical and empirical perspectives, allowing a broader understanding of the topics.

The book is complementary reading for textbooks, due to the objectivity with which it addresses important and quotidian issues in the region, associating empirical and theoretical topics, and facilitating the understanding of the international political economy of Latin America. It is also suitable for practitioners and researchers, because of the depth in which it covers specific topics and the useful analysis it conducts to incorporate policy implications and suggestions for achieving equitable growth in a context of liberal markets.

Gerardo Angeles-Castro received his PhD in economics from the University of Kent, UK. He is a consultant advisor at Tecnópoli and a research economist in the School of Economics at the Instituto Politécnico Nacional, Mexico. He is also a member of the National Researchers System, CONACYT, Mexico. His research interests include economic development, applied econometrics, international political economy, and transport economics.

Routledge Studies in Development Economics

For more information about this series, please visit: www.routledge.com/series/SE0266

Economic Liberalisation in Latin America

Gerardo Angeles-Castro

Routledge
Taylor & Francis Group

LONDON AND NEW YORK

First published 2021
by Routledge
2 Park Square, Milton Park, Abingdon, Oxon OX14 4RN

and by Routledge
52 Vanderbilt Avenue, New York, NY 10017

Routledge is an imprint of the Taylor & Francis Group, an informa business

British Library Cataloguing in Publication Data
A catalogue record for this book is available from the British Library

Library of Congress Cataloging-in-Publication Data
A catalog record has been requested for this book

ISBN: 978-0-367-45654-2 (hbk)
ISBN: 978-1-003-02456-9 (ebk)

Typeset in Times New Roman
by Taylor & Francis Books

To my wife Elodie

My sons Etienne Tonatiuh and Alexis Tenoch

My parents Alicia and Roberto

Contents

Illustrations

Figures

Tables

Acknowledgements

I gratefully acknowledge Oscar Manuel Gutierrez Valdes for assisting in the transcription of an early version of the manuscript, and three anonymous referees for their valuable comments. Usual disclaimers apply.

Introduction

Latin America has been characterised by a high degree of inequality since independence in the nineteenth century and even before; absolute poverty has also been largely endemic. During the post-war period, the import substitution industrialisation (lSI) model, supported by economic protectionism and state corporatism, failed to correct inequality. Moreover, in the early 1980s the model reached its limits and triggered an economic crisis that lasted most of the decade.

Escalating external debt and balance of payment difficulties during the 1980s moved most of the countries in the region toward negotiations with International Financial Institutions (IFIs). Such negotiations comprised adjustment programmes and conditionality. The set of policies that IFIs thought would be good for Latin America was labelled as the Washington Consensus (WC). It provided new perspectives for achieving economic growth, poverty alleviation, and income redistribution on the basis of market-oriented reforms with solid foundations in neoclassical theory. Furthermore, it advocates notions of democracy so as to provide social and political stability propitious for the operation of markets. This neoliberal approach has been challenged by an intensive critique since it is deemed an incomplete model that requires complementary strategies.

The WC in Latin America has shown a range of limitations and contradictions and has not met its initial expectations. This is one of the causes that encouraged a reformist agenda on a global scale by the late 1990s. In this context, multilateral institutions added social and human capital formation, civil society participation in a top-down sense, transparency and accountability, and institution building to the early elements of the WC in order to legitimise and humanise global economic liberalisation; this set of sociopolitical norms, incorporated into the original orthodoxy, was called the Post-Washington Consensus (PWC).[1]

Countries in the subcontinent adopted PWC polices to different extents; some cases hardly incorporated this model and they remained more attached to the original economic norms advocated by the WC, while a few countries even improved the sociopolitical prescription. Moreover, the introduction of market openness policies has also been diverse, as some countries adopted them with no restrictions while others involved regulatory policies and strategic state intervention at different levels in their economic policy.

This book is aimed at exploring the different economic liberalisation paths that Latin American countries have followed, the socioeconomic results the countries achieved according to the policies they implemented, and the challenges they face within a context of economic liberalisation. The analysis is conducted by looking at four country case studies: Mexico, Brazil, Chile, and Uruguay; they all represent different styles in the ways they have undertaken economic liberalisation, under different sociopolitical conditions and forms of social integration from the 1980s to recent years. In this book, the performance of the countries is also assessed in terms of economic growth, poverty alleviation, and income distribution at an early stage following economic liberalisation, and over the long run.

The four country case studies encompass the most representative economic liberalisation paths in the region. They range from models strongly attached to the WC economic norms with little social emphasis to models involving strategic restrictions on trade, regulatory policies, as well as inclusive social policy and participatory democracy that overcome the prescription advocated by the PWC. Thus, the sample is representative of the diverse economic liberalisation process conducted in Latin America and provides important insights for the analysis.

The case of Mexico fits the original WC version and confirms that this model is not an option for attaining significant economic growth with poverty reduction and income distribution.

The Brazilian model has been described as *inclusive neoliberalism,* but is also deemed a case of unsustained trade openness, since it adopted some economic and stabilisation polices in line with the WC, and inclusive social policies consistent with the PWC, but in some episodes of macroeconomic imbalance reversed the trade liberalisation process, while keeping an emphasis on strategic trade openness. This set of policies managed to slightly reduce poverty and income inequality, and presented low and volatile rates of economic growth, especially as a result of the stabilisation policies.

The Chilean case is in keeping with a number of PWC characteristics, and it illustrates that this model is able to achieve substantial economic growth and poverty reduction. On the other hand, this country case also shows that its economic and social approach, consisting of strong reliance on comparative advantages, on the basis of natural resources and low wages, and a disproportional balance of power among social actors, is associated with persistent income inequality and lower levels of economic growth over the long run.

Uruguay is a case of social aggregation from below and resistance to economic liberalisation under conditions of real participatory democracy, but it is also a case of resistance to subtle market reforms. Under these circumstances this country has managed to keep inequality at lower levels than the other three countries studied here and to reduce poverty; however, it has also shown constrained rates of economic growth in some periods.

Regardless of the style (strategy or model) to conduct economic liberalisation and the sociopolitical conditions that have prevailed in the four country case studies, they all show persistent economic difficulties consisting of low tax revenue as a percentage of GDP, high informal employment, and volatile economic growth.

According to the country case studies, none of the market openness strategies offer a real alternative for Latin America. On the other hand, economic liberalisation is unlikely to be abandoned in the region; however, the Latin American state needs to undertake pragmatic and subtle openness, that is, strategic liberalisation with especial emphasis on strengthening domestic markets,[2] reducing economic volatility, and avoiding powerlessness of vulnerable sectors[3].

Furthermore, real participatory democracy and social incorporation from below are essential for achieving income distribution and a fair balance of power among social actors. Nevertheless, the state should reject clientelist forms of aggregation so as to avoid resistance to subtle market dynamics.

The state also needs to undertake broader participation in the economy since the country case studies demonstrate that market forces are not enough to adjust to predefined comparative advantages. Moreover, it is essential to create new comparative advantages oriented to large-scale industrialisation by means of developmental forms of organisation and Keynesian principles so as to achieve both sustained economic growth and more possibilities for income distribution.[4]

The balance of payments constrained growth model is another approach to illustrate the role of industrialisation to boost growth. In the model, industrialisation oriented to import substitution reduces the marginal propensity to import and increases the exports value; through this pattern, constraints in the balance of payments declines and economic growth is liberated.[5]

The Latin American economies historically have had a large propensity to import and persistent current account deficits; to some extent, this occurs because the economies and their exports mostly rely on primary production, while they import products with more value added. Therefore, it is essential for the Latin American economies to foster industrialisation under conditions of competition, productivity, efficiency, and transparency, without affecting public finance.

Economic growth volatility can be addressed through diversification of markets, reduction of heavy reliance on commodities and primary production, and regulation of flows of speculative investments. The last action requires regional consensus to avoid subcontinental competition for capturing investment flows and to achieve more bargaining power for the region in global markets.

The Latin American states need to consolidate the formal economy, implement mechanisms to increase tax revenue, and conduct progressive fiscal policies and progressive social expenditure; these actions can provide the basis for better income distribution and equitable social conditions.

Latin American countries, within a market openness context, also require regional policy consolidation so as to cope with problems of under-representation in global forums, unfair mechanisms of trade and investment, and global polarisation, that is, greater autonomy and bargaining power in a global scale. Moreover, regional convergence and cooperation might counteract US hegemony within the hemisphere in trade negotiations. As a result, the challenge of the state is not confined to a domestic scope since it also involves regional and global actions. To the extent that Latin America as a region converges in a single model, it will be more feasible to cope with global and inter-regional problems to achieve a fair position on a global scale, and to resist global convergence.[6]

This book is organised as follows: Chapter 1 outlines the transition from the ISI model to market-oriented reforms, it also comments on the theoretical foundations and assumptions of the neoliberal model and the arguments that critique this approach. Chapter 2 assesses the outcomes of the WC in Latin America and illustrates the causes that encouraged the emergence of the PWC besides its characteristics, weaknesses, and strengths. Chapter 3 provides relevant cases—Mexico, Brazil, Chile, and Uruguay—in order to assess the economic performance of four different models, WC, unsustained trade liberalisation, PWC, and resistance to liberalisation respectively adopted in the medium term, that is, the period comprising the mid-1980s and late 1990s. Chapter 4 illustrates the performance of economic growth, inequality, poverty, and additional economic and social indicators in the four country case studies, with a longer-run perspective, and discusses how this evolution can be associated with the socioeconomic model of every country. Finally, concluding remarks and policy options are provided.

Notes

1 For a discussion, see, for example, Richard Higgott, 'Contested Globalisation: the Changing Context and Normative Challenges', *Review of International Studies*, 26 (2000).
2 For a discussion about the risk of neglecting the growth of the domestic market in the liberalisation process, see William Robinson, 'Globalisation as a Macro-Structural-Historical Framework of Analysis: the Case of Central America', *New Political Economy*, 7:2 (2002), pp. 221–250.
3 For a discussion about how liberalised markets are a major cause of vulnerability and powerlessness, see Peadar Kirby, 'The World Bank or Polany: Markets, Poverty and Social well-being in Latin America', *New Political Economy*, 7:2 (2002), pp. 199–219.
4 Lessons from the ISI model suggest that state intervention in the economy and active industrial policy might yield negative results. However, under improved sociopolitical conditions and reinvigorated institutions, industrial policy and state intervention can provide better results. In addition, large-scale industrialisation in the ISI model was not capable of absorbing the full labour force, but complementing industrialisation with predefined comparative advantages can offer more possibilities for employment, sustained economic growth, and income redistribution.

5 The model was first published by Thirlwall (1979). Besides its analytical potential, the model can predict the long-term rate of growth of countries, through the income elasticity of demand for imports and the rate of exports growth. It is also known as the Thirlwall law, because it has been satisfactorily tested in several economies.

6 In this sense, Hay contends that regionalisation plays a crucial role in mediating and refracting tendencies towards convergence or divergence. Hence, he claims that we can expect to see intra-regional convergence even in a context of inter-regional divergence (Hay 2000, 520).

1 The emergence of the Washington Consensus in Latin America
Theoretical foundations and challenges

The collapse of the ISI model and its destabilising effects provided an intellectual climate favourable for market-oriented reforms. The set of policies deemed appropriate for Latin America was labelled as the Washington Consensus. This neoliberal approach has solid foundations in standard neoclassical theory. It offered different perspectives for achieving economic growth, poverty reduction, and better levels of income distribution through the operation of market forces and the mechanism of prices. Nevertheless, its theoretical foundations have been challenged by an intensive critique, especially in the academic sphere since they are deemed idealistic and unfeasible if they are not complemented by additional strategies. This chapter comments on the transition from the ISI model to market-oriented reforms. In addition, it explains the theoretical foundations of the neoliberal paradigm and offers a critical approach of their ideological assumptions.

From the import substitution industrialisation model to market-oriented reforms

Latin America has been characterised by a high degree of inequality since independence, and even before; absolute poverty has also been largely endemic. The structuralist theory, developed simultaneously in the 1950s by several economists and by the Economic Commission for Latin America (ECLA), placed the responsibility for this situation on long-term historical forces, on the world capitalist economy, and on dominant classes who benefit from these conditions.

According to the structuralist approach the world economy is composed of a core or centre of highly industrialised countries and an underdeveloped periphery, where the former is dominant over the latter and determines the conditions in which peripheral economies produce. Gilpin asserts that the heart of the argument is that:

> the nature of technical advance, cyclical price movements, and differences in demands for industrial goods and primary products cause a secular deterioration in the terms of trade for commodity exporters, that is,

deterioration of the prices the less developed countries receive for their commodity exports relative to the prices of the manufactured goods they import from developed countries.

(Gilpin 1987, 275)

Consequently, for structuralists, a liberal capitalist world economy tends to preserve or actually increase inequalities between developed and less developed economies through mechanisms of trade and investment.

The core-periphery structure is maintained not just by the capitalist world system, but also by support from dominant classes, elites, or the ruling class in the periphery economies who benefit from the relationship and have an interest in perpetuating underdevelopment. These privileged classes maintain their internal position by exclusion or manipulation of the domestic social forces from economic or political power. For his part, Cox points out that within the periphery economies, a minority of labour employed in foreign-owned enterprises is integrated into the world economy, while the mass of local labour remains relatively deprived (Cox 1992, 174). Thus, the structuralist theory asserts that the world economy not only increases inequalities between developed and developing countries but also maintains social inequality in the periphery and neglects the true needs of the masses.

Structuralists have pointed out several policies to deal with these problems. The most important course of action advocated is rapid industrialisation in order to overcome the periphery's declining terms of trade and to absorb its labour surplus. Therefore, peripheral economies should pursue an import substitution strategy through policies of economic protectionism.[1] The ISI model prevailed in Latin America from the 1950s up to the early 1970s; during this period, the region experienced rapid industrialisation, high rates of economic growth, and improvement of the terms of trade. Furthermore, economic growth was associated with a fall in poverty. However, despite a drop in poverty, the long pattern of unequal income was prevalent in this epoch.[2]

Oxhorn outlines that the ISI model in Latin America was associated with state corporatism, since elites in control of the state saw this system of interest intermediation as their solution to their developmental problems. He claims that state corporatist institutions encouraged populist coalitions between the growing working class and the developmental state through hierarchical institutions that could effectively moderate workers' demands. According to Oxhorn, organised labour became a relatively privileged group, at the same time that its own interests were always subordinated to those of the dominant class. State corporatism became a fundamental component of process of controlled inclusion. On the other hand, people outside the modern industrial sector of the economy were generally denied economic and political power (Oxhorn 1999, 197–198). Hence, the model created economic polarisation between privileged groups and people outside them.

Critics of the ISI model suggest that the nature of the strategy worsens income distribution. Frank claims that the model involves capital-intensive techniques, so employment is low, as are wages, leaving a large part of the population marginalised, either unemployed or in traditional low productivity activities (quoted in Brewer 1990, 172). From this viewpoint, Gilpin asserts that the ISI strategy failed to produce sustained economic growth in less developed countries because the traditional social and economic conditions remained intact. Indeed, he argues that the neo-colonialist alliance of indigenous feudal elites with international capitalism has been reinforced by the ISI strategy. The result was an increased misdistribution of income and domestic demand too weak to sustain continued industrialisation (Gilpin 1987, 283).

Although the ISI model encouraged poverty reduction and achieved relatively high rates of economic growth for several years, the role of state corporatism and the nature of the model did not allow for tackling the pattern of unequal distribution of income. Furthermore, by the mid-1970s the model had showed symptoms of depletion. Substantial fiscal and trade deficits, income concentration, capital flights, weak domestic markets, but especially high rates of indebtedness and inflation disrupted economic growth. In addition, protectionism, clientelism, and corruption associated with state corporatism and authoritarianism exacerbated problems of inefficiency and waste. By the early 1980s the ISI model had reached its limits and created a severe economic crisis that lasted most of the decade.

For most of the 1980s Latin America struggled with the aftermath of the debt crisis; overall GDP per capita fell by 11 per cent, real wages declined, and unemployment and underemployment sharply increased (Morley 1995, 41). Furthermore, the Economic Commission for Latin America and the Caribbean (ECLAC) estimates that in 1990, 41 per cent of Latin Americans were living in poverty and 18 per cent were indigent.[3] By comparison, ten years earlier (in 1980), only 35 per cent were poor and just 15 per cent were indigent (ECLAC 1997, 28). It is worth noting that income distribution was also seriously affected. World Bank data for 18 Latin American countries indicate that the Gini coefficient rose from 0.45 in 1980 to 0.50 in 1989[4] (quoted in Robinson 1999, 49).

In short, the collapse of the ISI strategy and the debt crisis of the 1980s showed that this developmental model failed to produce sustained economic growth. Moreover, the so-called lost decade erased some of the improvements registered in the 1960s and 1970s, especially in terms of employment, poverty, real wages, and per-capita income. In addition, major shifts in income distribution were not registered during the successful years of the model, and degrees of inequality were regressive in the 1980s. Under these circumstances, it became clear to Latin American states that they needed to undertake deep and radical socioeconomic reforms, which placed greater emphasis on outward-oriented strategies.

The neoliberal model

Theoretical foundations

The failures of the ISI model provided an intellectual climate favourable to market-oriented reforms. Moreover, the strong influence that technocratic groups and epistemic communities exerted on Latin American governments, and the conditionality that multilateral institutions attached to their loans, led to a shift in the development paradigm after the mid-1980s towards a neoliberal model in which inward-looking development was replaced by export-led growth and state intervention by market forces.

John Williamson is given credit for first labelling 'the Washington Consensus'—the resulting agenda and the set of policy reforms which most of the multilateral financial institutions based in Washington thought would be good for Latin American countries.[5] This prescription divides policy reform into ten areas. Hojman outlines these ten areas as follows: fiscal discipline, public expenditure priorities, tax reform, financial liberalisation, market-determined exchange rates, trade liberalisation, foreign direct investment, privatisation, deregulation, and property rights (Hojman 1994, 193).

The neoliberal ideological consensus has solid foundations in familiar neoclassical trade theory, which argues that the welfare gains from free trade are unambiguous. FitzGerald points out that in the neoclassical argument, adjustment to world prices would allow resources to be allocated more efficiently and growth to be maximised. Cheaper natural resources and labour (in the case of Latin America) would be used more intensively as exports and imports adjust to comparative advantages and costly scarce capital would be used less. Exports and output would grow more rapidly, while trade would balance through a variable exchange rate (FitzGerald 1996, 32). In this sense, the Heckscher-Ohlin theory stresses that the freeing of trade should shift factor demand in favour of unskilled labour and agriculture in the lest developed countries (LDCs) and thereby improve the distribution of income (Berry 1998b, 3). Accordingly, in increasing trade based on comparative advantages, peasants' and low-skilled workers' income should expand relative to capital returns, since the demand for their service will rise and income would be redirected away from the scarce factor and toward the abundant factor. In this way, Tanski and French claim that within the neoclassical framework, trade liberalisation has a greater distributive effect between capital and labour, and increases competitiveness and reduces the tendency toward concentration of wealth (Tanski and French 2001, 678).

Barrett states that in the neoliberal view, efforts to increase the organisational capacity and bargaining power of labour through state-enforced labour standards pose an inherent threat to accumulation and economic efficiency. This is because they are seen as a drain on savings and investment and a source of labour market rigidity. Moreover, he emphasises that from this approach, it is only by limiting union power and allowing wages and the supply of labour to respond flexibly to market signals that sustained growth will be achieved (Barrett 2001, 563). A dynamic and flexible labour market helps to reallocate resources, to encourage international investment, and to improve competitiveness. Labour market adjustment includes legislation to reduce the power of labour unions, reduction in the number of public servants, reduction in the legislated minimum wages, and reduction of employers' contributions to various benefits for workers. Thomas asserts that in the short term these policies are likely to involve a net transfer from labour to capital and make the distribution of income more unequal. However, in the long term, freeing the labour market of distortions improves the distribution of income because it encourages employment expansion and wage increases in the poorest segments of society (Thomas 1996, 79, 86, 87).

In the neoliberal model, the package of fiscal, monetary, exchange, and related measures is intended to achieve macroeconomic stability, an essential requisite for the operation and free mobility of capital. The liberalisation of trade and finance, privatisation of public enterprises, and the opening of the capital account create the preconditions for large capital flows from abroad. Such foreign flows are welcomed because they supplement domestic savings and investments and therefore boost growth. Griffith-Jones argues that in the neoliberal perspective, portfolio equity and FDI emerge as a new source of finance which reduces commercial bank lending; furthermore, foreign capital inflows encourage the lowering of domestic real interest rates. In this view, government expenditure going to external and domestic debt servicing declines significantly and there is room for fairly large increased spending on the social sectors that benefit the poorer sections of society (Griffith-Jones 1996, 129, 139, 140). Hence, for neoliberals the impact of capital surges reduces income inequality and poverty.

For Neoliberals, through outward oriented reforms, income dispersion may widen and absolute poverty increases in the short-term. However, they argue that the market will react and their operations and the mechanism of prices cause resources to be reallocated; in addition, economic growth provides resources for poverty alleviation, but meanwhile the model suggests that social assistance can be used to provide targeted safety nets. In this context Vilas asserts that the neoliberal social policy is a set of measures oriented to compensate the negative effects of macroeconomic adjustments and market distortions. This policy is cyclical and is not permanent. Once economic growth and employment are reactivated, social programmes can be suspended, since the market forces can conduct the efficient allocation of resources. He also claims that neoliberal social programmes are not aimed at social development as the notion of the state intervention becomes redundant and misleading in the long-run; therefore, social policy is rather oriented to avoid further poverty and to assist the victims of the adjustment only during the transition process or during recessive periods (Vilas 1997, 934–935).

Robinson underlines that the political component of the neoliberal structural adjustment is to make the world safe for capital. It requires developing social controls and political institutions most propitious for achieving a stable world environment; furthermore, it requires promoting democracy in order to secure the best conditions for international capital accumulation (Robinson 2000, 312–313). The theoretical foundation of this position is classical modernisation theory.[6] According to Panizza (2000, 737), this approach holds that economic modernisation will bring about an autonomous state capable of enforcing the universal rule of law, representative political institutions and a political culture of rights and accountability. Moreover, in classical modernisation theory, it is emphasised that liberal democracy and economic liberalism go hand in hand and that the former is the outcome of economic development. In the neoliberal approach, therefore, democracy provides political and social stability, which is essential for international capital flows and for the achievement of economic development. Poverty alleviation and better income distribution in such circumstances can be attained.

The neoliberal model takes the liberal assertion that failure to develop is ascribed to domestic market imperfections and improper government policies such as a weak financial system, substantial fiscal deficits, and overvalued currencies.[7] In this sense, Gilpin asserts that for liberal economists, development requires the removal of political and social obstacles such as political corruption and parasitic social and bureaucratic structure (Gilpin 1987, 266–267). Whereas structuralists maintain that underdevelopment is caused by external forces of the world capitalist system, liberals find the obstacles to development within the less developed countries themselves.

The neoliberal model offered a new perspective for achieving poverty reduction and better levels of income distribution in Latin America. Nevertheless, its theoretical foundations have been challenged by an intensive critique, especially in the academic sphere. The critical view and limitations of this approach are addressed in the following section.

Challenges

The neoliberal postulates and particularly the Washington Consensus prescription have been broadly criticised in the literature; sometimes they are labelled as idealistic and unfeasible. Growth and development, democratic consolidation, and income distribution are three factors that are deemed difficult to achieve under neoliberal policies without the implementation of complementary strategies.

Economic perspective

In the neoliberal prescription, trade liberalisation is accompanied by capital account liberalisation, which creates the conditions for large capital flows from abroad and a tendency toward exchange rate appreciation, a rapid reduction in trade surplus, and an increase in the current account deficit. Revaluation discourages exports, raises imports, and thus undermines the logic of the model, which is based on export-led growth. This may crowd out domestic industry and existing activities, and may have negative long-term effects on output and employment. As a result, poverty and income distribution could worsen.

The new development model seeks to achieve a comparative advantage for Latin America through natural resources and labour-intensive manufacturing based on cheap labour. In this respect, the New-Keynesian approach states that reliance on natural resources and weak industrialisation does not form the basis for sustained exports growth. Consequently, income dispersion and absolute poverty increase due to slow rates of growth, lack of skilling, and depressed wages. FitzGerald outlines that in the New-Keynesian approach successful export growth depends upon specific government intervention, particularly in order to support corporate investment, technological innovation, and labour skilling. In addition, according to the model, an appropriate industrialisation fosters economic growth, employment, and higher wages, and provides better results for income distribution (FitzGerald 1996 34, 35). The balance of payments constrained growth model (Thirlwall 1979) also stresses the role of industrialisation and import substitution to reduce the income elasticity of demand for imports, increase exports, avoid persistent current account deficit, and eventually, boost economic growth.

The economic success of the East Asian countries has undermined neo-liberal assumptions. New industrialised countries (NICs) are usually associated with the concept of the developmental state. According to Pempel:

> developmental states [...] actively and regularly intervene in economic activities with the goal of improving the international competitiveness of their domestic economies. Rather than accepting some predefined places in a world divided on the basis of 'comparative advantages' such states seek to create 'competitive advantages'.
>
> (Pempel 1999, 139).

Moreover, in order to absorb labour and finance welfare provision, developmental states seek to achieve higher value-added activities and large-scale industrialisation, by means of industrial policy, human capital formation, and technological development. In this way, NICs have not only attained rapid and sustained economic growth, but have also achieved unusually low levels of inequality (World Bank 1993, 28–32). Hence, the WC did not take into account the benefits that emerged from developmental strategies.

In the view of Barrett, the nature of the neoliberal model implies that 'the more reliant a country is on trade, the weaker the link between consumption and production and the more the wages tend to be seen as a cost of production rather than a source of demand' (Barrett 2001, 594). In contrast, under a Keynesian approach there is room for improving labour standards given the importance of demand to that model. In this respect, Barrett claims that labour market flexibility is an insufficient basis for competitiveness and economic growth and may be counterproductive since it limits domestic market (*loc. cit.*).

From the New-Keynesian perspective, depressed wages and structural unemployment lead to a fall in domestic demand, which inhibit recovery and sustained economic growth not only in the short run but also in the long run, and increase income dispersion and absolute poverty (FitzGerald 1996, 34). The fact that the neoliberal model considers global capital growth as the main cause of development and welfare (instead of domestic market growth) has negative implications for capital accumulation and income distribution.

When exchange rate policy gradually shifts away from support for the opening up of the economy and towards the control of inflation, appreciation keeps rising (Agosin et al. 1995, 22). As a result, revaluation may discourage exports and expand imports. Moreover, high domestic real interest rates may be used to attract foreign capital, which discourages real investment and exacerbates the government deficit. Furthermore, if the principal component of capital inflows is foreign portfolio investment (FPI), there is an implicit risk of volatility and reduced possibilities of productive investment, which could be the cause of an abrupt reduction or even a large reversal of capital inflows. In such circumstances, it is likely to have negative long-term effects on output and macroeconomic stability, and regressive effects in terms of income distribution.

Privatisation and foreign capital inflows lead to a rapid expansion of the bond and equity markets and encourage price increases of existing stocks rather than increases in the quantity of bonds and equities, which indicates a higher concentration of capital. When privatisation is conducted within a policy of increasing the number of individuals and enterprises participating in the stock market, capital concentration is not reduced significantly since asset holders are usually concentrated in the upper income class.

Privatisation of state-owned firms and liberalisation of FDI encourage a surge of mergers and acquisitions across borders and tend to create dominant positions and oligopolistic markets. This undermines one of the basic liberal propositions: competitive markets. In addition, this likely pattern decreases the market power of small and medium-sized enterprises (SMEs) and leads to deterioration of domestic industry, and capital concentration.

When FDI is disembedded from the local economy and is not open to linkages with local suppliers, the wage and output multiplier effect is small (Tanski and French 2001, 678). Moreover, FDI could add growth simply by crowding in domestic investment (the process in which FDI boosts domestic investment by creating links with domestic firms and industries); however, if FDI crowds out equal or larger amounts of investment from domestic sources by competing in product and financial markets, effects for economic growth and welfare could be adverse (Borensztein et al. 1998, 128). From this perspective, an aggressive liberalisation of FDI that does not complement and foster domestic industry could depress employment and wages, and affect income distribution.

According to Bailey, Harte and Sugden, the race to attract new inward investment via fiscal policies, that is, subsidy packages and downward pressure on corporation taxes, results in an evaporating tax base, which decreases the scope for redistributive and social expenditure by governments (Bailey et al. 1998, 296). In this way, decreasing social expenditure can have negative effects on economic growth and income redistribution.

Democratic and social perspective

From Robinson's viewpoint, transition from authoritarianism and dictatorship, in which interaction and economic integration on a world scale are obstructed, to a more consensually based system and a minimally stable environment for global capitalism to operate, represented a crisis of elite rule and an effort by transnational, dominant groups to reconstitute hegemony through a change in the mode of political domination (Robinson 1999, 59–60). Under the rubric of democracy, this crisis was resolved through transitions to polyarchies. They offered transnational elites the opportunity to create a more favourable institutional framework for a deepening of neoliberal adjustment. According to Robinson, 'polyarchy refers a system in which a small group actually rules and mass participation in decision-making is confined to leadership choice in elections carefully managed and dominated by competing elites' (Robinson 2000, 310).

Within polyarchies, basically state elites and privileged groups in society are involved in the decision-making process. Therefore, real participatory democracy that includes the active role of different sectors of civil society in the decision-making process in a bottom-up sense, social democracy that promotes a redistributive project, or local democracy that respects the dignity and individuality of community members is not consolidated and is not always central in the national agenda.

In order to achieve rapid and aggressive structural changes, propitious for the operation of private capital, neoliberal democracies can evolve into a type of democracy requiring some form of electoral legitimating of executive authority. Such legitimating is consistent with the kind of authoritarian concentration of executive power that O'Donnell has labelled 'delegative democracy' (DD), which 'rest[s] on the premise that whoever wins the election for the presidency is entitled to govern as he or she sees fit, constrained only by the hard facts of existing power relations and by a constitutionally limited term of office' (quoted in Panizza 2000, 738). Moreover, it is also consistent with authoritarian concentration of executive power, what Oxhorn (1999, 207) calls 'hyper-presidentialism'.

The neoliberal model privileging accumulation does not require an inclusionary social base; in such circumstances, it is unclear whether polyarchy or DD can be maintained in the long run. In this respect, Robinson holds that 'socioeconomic exclusion is inherent in the model since accumulation does not depend on a domestic market or internal social production. The neoliberal model generates political tensions—inequality, polarization, impoverishment, and marginality—conductive to a breakdown of polyarchy' (Robinson 1999, 60). The logic of neoliberalism and neoliberal democracy in the long run leads to incompatibility between capital accumulation and wealth since social polarisation can generate mass conflicts that jeopardise economic and political stability, and hence inhibits sustained economic growth and income distribution.

Social programmes aimed at reducing inequity tend to be small because of persisting fiscal stringency, austerity measures, and cutbacks in social expenditure. Furthermore, social programmes are not subject to democratic controls or do not operate under the logic of effective participatory democracy due to the nature of neoliberal democracy. As a consequence, they tend to be implemented under political manipulation of social spending. Robinson stresses that social policy programmes that operate within the logic of the neoliberal model are conducted as temporary relief to those marginalised by the economic adjustment, but without modifying the structural causes of that marginalisation (Robinson 1999, 66). From this viewpoint, they are not enough to reverse the regressive impact on income distribution and to ameliorate the spread of poverty that emerges in the economic adjustment.

After the implementation of the Washington Consensus reforms in Latin America, it can be assessed whether they have performed, in terms of income distribution and poverty reduction, according to the assumptions of their theoretical foundations, or have been unfeasible as their critics predict. The outcomes of the neoliberal model in Latin America in an early stage, between the mid-1980s and the late 1990s, which is the period of adjustment and WC reforms, are the area of study in Chapter 2. Moreover, it provides the analysis of the transition from WC to PWC as a result of the perceived failure of the former.

Notes

1 Helleiner claims that some scholars, e.g. Gilpin, have associated nationalism to the logic of protectionism and statism. In this way the ISI model could be considered a nationalist strategic. However, this position has been contested since nationalism can be associated with a wide range of policy projects, including liberal policies (Helleiner 2002, 307–329).

2 In this respect, Berry points out that over the period 1950–1980 the region's per capita income rose by about 3 per cent per year; in addition, he asserts that poverty incidence was about 25 per cent of households in 1980, whereas he suggests that poverty incidence in 1950 had been around 65 per cent. Nevertheless, most countries of the region did not witness major shifts in income distribution in this period (Berry 1998a, 13).

3 The poverty line is defined by the United Nations as twice the cost of a minimally adequate food basket, as determined by the nutritional standards of the World Health Organization (WHO). Indigence, a more extreme form of poverty, is defined as an income that fails to meet even the cost of a basic food basket (United Nations 2002).

4 Gini coefficients is a summary measure of the extent to which the actual distribution of income or consumption differs from a hypothetical uniform distribution in which each person or household receives an identical share. The Gini coefficient has a maximum value of 1, indicating that one person or household receives everything, and a minimum value of zero, indicating absolute equality. James W. Wilkie, Eduardo Aleman, and José Guadalupe Ortega., 'Statistical Abstract of Latin America', 38, (Los Angeles: Latin American Center Publications, University of California, 2002). p. 446.

5 The components of the Washington Consensus are listed in John Williamson 'What Washington Means by Policy Reform', in John Williamson, eds., *Latin American Adjustment: How Much Has Happened?* (Washington DC: Institute for International Economics, 1990), pp. 7–20.

6 Lipset is given credit for the classic formulation of modernisation theory: Seymour Martin Lipset, *Political Man* (London: Heinemann, 1960).

7 For a discussion about the liberal perspective on economic development, see Robert Gilpin, *The Political Economy of International Relations.* (Princeton, Oxford: Princeton University Press, 1987), pp. 265–270.

2 Implications of the Washington Consensus reforms and resulting trends

The outcomes of the neoliberal model between the mid-1980s and late 1990s in Latin America—the period of reforms and early operation of market-oriented policies—were more consistent with the arguments of their critics, since the initial expectations of Washington Consensus (WC) reforms were not met. Economic growth was modest, whereas poverty and income inequality among the population remained important problems to be tackled. Hence, this development paradigm resulted in an incomplete model that required complementary strategies. As a consequence, the Post-Washington Consensus (PWC) added a set of sociopolitical norms to the original neo-liberal model, and attempted to humanise market dynamics. The prescription provides better conditions for economic growth and poverty alleviation. Nevertheless, it still has limitations in terms of income distribution and sustained economic expansion. This chapter assesses the initial outcomes of the neoliberal reforms and comments on the characteristics and limitations of the PWC.

The liberalisation process and its impact on Latin America

Economic context

Latin American trade liberalisation programmes were conducted rapidly. In this sense, Agosin and French-Davis (1995, 10–20)[1] assert that in most of the cases import liberalisation was carried out over a period of just two to three years, entailing destruction of existing installed capacity. Hence, in Latin America, results were less positive from those expected. In fact, FitzGerald (1996, 42–48) emphasises that imports grew faster than exports and the economy was largely based on limited primary export markets and cheap labour, with insufficient attention paid to industrial export promotion.

Although Latin America has tended to exploit comparative advantages based on natural resources and cheap labour, FitzGerald contends that the jobs created by the growth rates in exports were not sufficiently greater than labour force growth rates and import-competing job losses. As a result, wage dispersion increased due to the oversupply of unskilled labour. Then, the region presented little potential for dynamic economic growth and income redistribution (ibid., 40–49).

Both trade and capital account liberalisation in Latin America were accompanied or often preceded by domestic capital market and FDI deregulation. As the neoliberal approach predicts, this created the preconditions for large capital flows from abroad.[2] For the region as a whole, the entry of capital contributed to the recovery of economic growth since the annual rate increased from 1.6 per cent in 1983–1990 to 3.4 per cent in 1991–1993 (ibid., 132).

The speed of capital inflows was reflected in increasing exchange rate appreciation and the current account deficit. According to ECLAC, of 18 countries in Latin America and the Caribbean, 16 experienced exchanged rate appreciation between 1990 and mid-1994 (quoted in ibid., 137). In addition, the dominance of speculative financial flows over productive capital raised the issue of potential volatility of the economy. Moreover, domestic and external shocks triggered the stability of such flows. Under these circumstances, the surge of capital inflows could not be sustained indefinitely. The 1994–1995 Mexican crisis signalled a large reversal of capital inflows across the region; furthermore, the crisis had contagious effects in other countries of the hemisphere—notably Argentina.[3] Therefore, the capital inflow boom of the early 1990s gave an illusion of recovery, while the dominance of speculative financial flows did not generate conditions for substantial new employment opportunities and sustained economic growth. In this context, Griffith-Jones (1996, 141) argues that the rapid inflows of capital and the abrupt reversal of such flows increased income inequality and poverty. This effect was particularly strong because the inflows did not lead to a significant increase in investment in tradeables and production.

Volatile capital inflows and excessively overvalued exchange rates led to prolonged and repetitive episodes of financial crisis involving collateral effects and contagion across the region—Brazil in 1998–1999 is worth noting.[4] These episodes undermined economic growth and income distribution.

Democratic and social context

As has been commented on, in the transition toward neoliberalism there is an implicit risk since the crisis of elite rules can be solved by the adoption of polyarchies or delegative democracies (DDs). Indeed, Latin America did not escape this risk. During the late 1980s and early 1990s a number of presidents introduced Washington Consensus reforms by means of authoritarian concentrations of executive authority.[5] By the same token, Latin American countries saw radical and authoritarian policy changes that led to political corruption, social polarisation, and restricted political participation.

This transformation generated mass conflicts, social movements, and uprisings seeking democratisation and an egalitarian outcome. For example, the Zapatist rebellion of Indigenous people in the Mexican state of Chiapas in

January of 1994 attempted to change the Mexican political system. Furthermore, social polarisation generated political tension that jeopardised economic stability. In fact, the Zapatist uprising in Mexico is deemed to be one of the domestic shocks generating uncertainty and massive outflows of capital which culminated in the currency crisis in late 1994.[6] Consequently, neoliberalism and neoliberal democracy in Latin America generated social conditions that inhibited political and economic stability and constrained sustained economic growth and the redistribution of income. The neoliberal model in Latin America and its inherent democratic systems did show serious contradictions for the stable operation of private capital, for the achievement of sustained economic growth, and for the implementation of an efficient redistributionist project.

The perceived slow economic growth, the depressed domestic market, and the reduction of corporation taxes inhibited a substantial expansion of tax revenue. In addition, social expenditure decreased because of the austerity programmes, aimed at reducing inflation and domestic consumption, and the subsides to inflows of foreign investment. As a result, Latin America faced structural weakness in the financing of social security provision, which reduced possibilities to counteract the structural causes of long-term inequality. On the other hand, although almost every country undertook social programmes, they were not big enough to dissipate destabilising political tension, or to compensate for the worsening distribution of income. These programmes were not successful because they operated as temporary relief for marginalised sectors; in some cases they were subjected to political manipulation (FONCADES in Peru and PRONASOL in Mexico)[7], and others had constrained economic resources.

Statistical evidence

According to the information illustrated in Table 2.1, between the mid-1980s and the late 1990s, the years of adjustment and implementation of WC reforms in Latin America, only five of 14 countries reduced their urban Gini coefficient. Eight of 14 countries reduced the proportion of urban households below the poverty line; Table 2.1 also shows that the whole region did not change this indicator during the period. In addition, ECLAC (2002, 38, 71) points out that between 1986 and 1997 the proportion of rural and urban households below the poverty line in the region hardly changed; it moved from 37 per cent to 36 per cent. ECLAC also notes that between 1990 and 1999 only four of 15 countries improved their total Gini coefficient. These statistics illustrate the regressive trends in income distribution and the lack of improvements in poverty alleviation along structural reforms in Latin America.

Within these adverse results there is some room for domestic explanations. The economics of liberalisation was implemented by the old politics; consequently, political inefficiency, corruption, and authoritarianism were inherited

Table 2.1 Income distribution and poverty indicators, selected years 1984–1998, urban population

Country	Year	Gini Coefficient	Households below the poverty line (percentage)
Argentina	1986	0.406	—
	1990	0.423	12
	1997	0.439	12
Bolivia	1989	0.484	49
	1992	0.467	45
	1997	0.455	47
Brazil	1990	0.528	36
	1996	0.538	25
Chile	1990	0.471	33
	1998	0.474	17
Colombia	1986	0.455	36
	1990	0.450	35
	1997	0.477	19
Costa Rica	1988	0.364	21
	1990	0.345	22
	1997	0.357	17
Ecuador	1990	0.381	56
	1997	0.388	50
El Salvador	1995	0.382	40
	1997	0.384	49
Honduras	1986	—	53
	1990	0.487	65
	1997	0.448	67
Mexico	1984	0.321	28
	1992	0.414	30
	1998	0.405	31
Panama	1986	0.430	30
	1991	0.448	34
	1997	0.462	25
Paraguay	1986	0.404	—
	1994	—	42

Table 2.1 (continued)

Country	Year	Gini Coefficient	Households below the poverty line (percentage)
	1996	0.389	40
Uruguay	1986	0.385	14
	1990	0.353	12
	1997	0.300	6
Venezuela	1986	0.384	25
	1990	0.378	33
	1997	0.425	42
LatinAmerica	1986	—	30
	1990	—	35
	1997	—	30

Source: Wilkie et al. (2002), Tables 1411 and 1416

from the era of state corporatism and exacerbated social inequity. Furthermore, countries with macroeconomic disequilibria and government failures such as high fiscal deficits, fixed exchanges rates, and weak financial systems were more vulnerable. Indeed, the Mexican and Brazilian crises were associated with inadequate banking supervision and lack of transparency on the one hand, and distortions of macroeconomic fundamentals on the other. However, the market panic and the markets' reaction that characterised both economic collapses were excessive and exaggerated to the extent of macroeconomic fundamentals they faced. Accordingly, the increasing income inequality in Latin America in the period of analysis was the result of rapid and excessive liberalisation under conditions of domestic inefficiency in some cases.

The range of limitations of the neoliberal model in Latin America was one of the causes that encouraged the emergence of a reformist agenda on a global scale. The elements and objectives of this consensus are analysed in the following section.

The Post-Washington Consensus

Causes and characteristics

Spreading currency crises in emerging markets in the 1990s (e.g. Mexico, the Asia region, Russia, and Brazil) were associated with the surge of capital flows following wide-scale liberalisation. This fact represents a reason to reconsider aspects of globalisation.

Higgott shows statistical evidence about the increasing global income gaps between 1960 and 1995 and points out the emerging evidence to suggest the existence of a causal relationship between inequality and global liberalisation; he argues that resistance to globalisation developed during the 1990s (Higgott 2000, 135–136). Global resistance was strengthened by local bottom-up movements of civil society in different regions of the world as a counterweight to hegemonic power and ideology.

Crises in emerging markets, increasing global inequality, the poor results achieved in Latin America, and the international and local sites of resistance to globalisation demonstrated that the neoliberal project had fallen into a deep crisis by the end of the decade and reinforced the need to move beyond the initial consensus.

International Financial Institutions recognised the destabilising effects of the architecture of the WC and the growing perception that it exacerbates inequity. From this perspective, Higgott stresses that the WC was insufficiently flexible to respond to what he calls 'new politics of contested globalisation'. As a consequence, this led to the end of the hegemony of that neoliberal orthodoxy that dominated the 1980s and 1990s and the emergence of a Post-Washington Consensus (ibid., 137). This approach added civil society participation, social and human capital formation, effective democratic regulation, transparency and accountability, and institution building to the market-oriented economic policies advocated by the original WC. It is an attempt to humanise the operation of market forces and politically legitimise the early elements of the WC in order to quell resistance to global economic liberalisation.

These themes emerged and were adopted by different multilateral institutions. The World Bank's 1997 development report, 'The State in a Changing World', is a key document in explaining this thinking. It advocates that poverty reduction and sustainable development require five crucial ingredients: 1) a foundation of law and property rights; 2) public investment in infrastructure, and public investment in people, including health and education with special attention to basic schooling; 3) protection of the vulnerable through programmes of social assistance, and social insurance programmes such as pension and unemployment; 4) protection of the natural environment; and 5) a benign policy environment, including macroeconomic stability, avoiding price distortion, and liberalising trade and investment (World Bank 1997, 41). With reference to the last point, it is interesting to note that the World Bank highlights the desirability of prudential regulation, supervision, and relaxed controls in areas such as banking and short-run investment in order to cope with financial turbulence (ibid., 65, 135); nevertheless, economic liberalisation is deemed essential for growth.

In the realm of industrial policy, the report recognises that there is no 'once-size-fits-all formula'. In addition, the report distinguishes between institution-intensive and institution-light approaches to industrial policy and claims that the former requires strong administrative capability in order to be successful, but asserts that activist industrial policy has often been a recipe for disaster. As a result, it lays out the desirability of reinvigorating institutions for a capable public sector and restraining arbitrary state action and corruption. On the other hand, for the report, industrial policy means fostering private to private collaboration and working in partnership with firms and citizens. Moreover, it emphasises that privatisation and liberalisation are the appropriate priorities for countries whose governments have been over-extended (ibid., 61–75); hence it seems to be reluctant to encourage countries to pursue industrial policies involving an active participation of the state in industrial issues.

The report considers electoral participation as the primary manifestation of citizen voice. However, it suggests an alternative participatory mechanism for informing and consulting, such as public–private deliberation between the government and non-governmental organisations (NGOs), civil society, business, and labour sectors on the one hand, and improving decentralisation and local accountability on the other (ibid., 111, 117–122).

In short, the report places special emphasis on social and political issues, and highlights economic liberalisation, privatisation, and light industrial policy as essential themes. Through this prescription, the report suggests that successful economic development rests on domestic and local policies, but it seems to neglect global actions as a means of improving economic development.

The World Bank's 2000–2001 development report, 'Attacking Poverty', goes further. It recognises the rising disparities between rich countries and the developing world, and outlines poverty as a global problem of huge proportions (World Bank 2001a, 3). It points out that global actions need to complement national and local activities to achieve maximum benefit for poor people throughout the world. Such global actions include expanding market access in high-income countries, reducing the risk of economic crises, encouraging the production of international public goods that benefit poor people, and ensuring a voice for poor countries and poor people in global forums (ibid., 179–188).

The collaboration of the UN in the new PWC rhetoric can be observed in the development of the Global Compact.[8] It was released in July 2000 and promotes a code of ethics among multinational corporations (MNCs) through a voluntary agreement that contains nine principles under three headings: human rights, labour, and environment. The global compact fits within a neoliberal discourse since it encourages interaction between the international institutions and the corporate world. In this sense, it does not attempt to obstruct flows of FDI across countries; nevertheless, it is a significant recognition of the need to globalise some important common values.

The International Labour Organization (ILO) responded to the new rhetoric through special emphasis on human and social capital formation. The 'World Employment Report 1998–99, Employability in the Global Economy: How Training Matters' asserts that there is increasing evidence to show the role of education levels as determinants of growth and poverty alleviation. In theoretical terms, this is explained by the so-called 'endogenous or new growth theories', which claim that the sources of differences in living standards among and within nations are in human capital. For the ILO, this leads to a policy in favour of government intervention going beyond compensating for market forces, to more deliberate public investment in education and training, especially primary education and low-skill training (International Labour Organization 1998, 119).

The ILO's 2000 report, 'Income Security and Social Protection in a Changing World', highlights that economic growth and market forces do not necessarily reduce poverty. Consequently, social protection and income security programmes are required for achieving major changes in society (International Labour Organization 2000, 224). The report not only asserts that mechanisms of social protection such as healthcare, pensions, benefits for parents and children, social assistance, and protection during incapacity and unemployment are essential, but also the desirability of extending the coverage of social protection, popular participation, and the need for good governance (ibid., 225–234). The ILO does not reject the original consensus; it rather attempts to socialise the economic model as a way of reconciling the neoliberal policies such as labour flexibilisation with strategies to address issues of social and human capital formation.

The set of polices advocated by the multilateral institutions illustrates the way the rhetoric of the PWC tries to consolidate the key norms of the WC on a global scale, since it does not reject emphasis on economic liberalisation. In addition, the PWC is an attempt to induce support for a new set of sociopolitical norms in order to legitimate the original consensus by acknowledging the need to mitigate its negative effects. This new development represented a further step toward the recognition of the importance of tackling poverty and the pursuit of efficient states with a social conscience. Nevertheless, the PWC has been challenged by a number of shortcomings.

Limitations

Economic polarisation and increasing poverty are two causes that inhibit economic stability and encourage revolts against globalisation. According to Weber, the objective of the poverty reduction agenda of the PWC was central to the making of what she identifies as an emerging 'global development architecture' (GDA) that pursues policy convergence in the logic of the unification movement, which has private international trade law as a central norm.

Moreover, she claims that a poverty reduction strategy resists the implementation of neoliberal policies, which allows the expansion of the global unification movement to the level of local communities. In these terms, the poverty reduction agenda under 'the PWC suggests an approach to development based on a strategy of crisis management. The objective seems to manage what is perceived as "two crises": the crisis of global poverty and the crisis of global capitalism' (Weber 2001, 4–10).

For Weber, disciplinary neoliberalism focuses on risk management at the community level that facilitates a 'top-down' adjustment from the 'bottom up' and legitimates coercive convergence; furthermore, this strategy is complemented at the global level by enhanced policy coordination. Under these circumstances, she argues that the political implications of development as crisis management may well be regressive, since it is aimed at delegitimating global social movements. In other words, genuine political struggle of development is undermined; moreover, this is equivalent to a 'social closure'. Hence, in the emerging GDA there is no room for contending routes of development (ibid., 25–26).

Although the PWC highlights poverty alleviation strategies as a means of legitimising economic liberalisation and avoiding resistance, the global distribution of wealth among and within countries is not a central part of the agenda for consideration. That is, income distribution takes a secondary role. This approach seems to accept capital accumulation and underestimates global polarisation that is exacerbated by the transnationalisation of market forces. However, a world that sustains significant levels of inequality is likely to be unstable.

In the PWC approach, the simple understanding of governance as the effective and efficient management of the modern state undermines both global democracy and the genuine recognition of ethical questions of justice. In Higgott's (2000, 143–148) viewpoint, the incorporation of civil society, non-state actors, and global social movements into the policy process is considered a necessary condition for the legitimation of the liberalising agenda. However, he claims that this form of collective action and incorporation does not solve the problem of under-representation of developing countries, nor their agendas for greater redistribution. In the formalised policy process, global governance issues are dominated by interest representations and alliance constructions between the powerful state groupings such as the G7 and international organisations. Moreover, neoliberalism remains the driving ideology with universalising notions of convergence. Hence, the vast majority of the world's population remain rule-takers. In this respect, Higgott outlines the lack of representative and democratic structures of global political space that allows a deliberative dialogue between rule-makers and rule-takers.

To the extent that development continues to be based on crisis management, the distribution of wealth remains a secondary concern, and global democracy fails to create a global public domain, economic liberalisation and the global governance agenda advocated by the PWC will become more contested and less feasible.[9]

The following chapter provides four country case studies: Mexico, Brazil, Chile, and Uruguay, whose development models tend to be compatible with: the WC, unsustained trade liberalisation, the PWC, and resistance to economic liberalisation, respectively, so as to evaluate their economic and sociopolitical results. These four country case studies help to assess weaknesses and strengths of four different trajectories of economic liberalisation, and their effect on income distribution, poverty, and economic growth, over the period in which market-oriented reforms were implemented and the early years of their operation.

Notes

1 By contrast, the opening of the NICs was a long state-led process involving construction of a production apparatus oriented toward international markets, while the liberalisation of imports played a secondary-supporting role (Agosin and French-Davis 1995, 10–20).

2 As a matter of fact, in the early 1990s a large surge of foreign capital flowed to the region; as a result, net capital flows expanded from US$ 10.1 to US$ 64.2 billion between 1989 and 1993 (Griffith-Jones 1996, 129).

3 For a discussion about the 1994–1995 exchange rate crisis in Mexico and Argentina, see Pamela K. Starr 'Capital Flows, Fixed Exchange Rates, and Political Survival: Mexico and Argentina, 1994–1995', in P. Oxhorn and P. Starr, eds., *Markets and Democracy in Latin America: Conflicto or Convergence?* (London: Lynne Rienner Publishers, 1999), pp. 203–238.

4 See, for example, Afonso Ferreira and Giuseppe Tullio, 'The Brazilian Exchange Rate Crisis of January 1999', *Journal of Latin American Studies*, 34 (2002), pp. 161–162.

5 Philip points out that Menem in Argentina packed the Supreme Court with his own supporters, whereas Fujimori went further still and closed Congress altogether in 1992. Moreover, he claims that the post-1989 democratic presidents of Chile ruled under the strongly presidentialist 1980 Constitution (Philip 1999, 235). In addition, Salinas in Mexico was supported by the hegemony of a single political party.

6 See Frederic S. Mishkin, 'Understanding Financial Crises: A Developing Country Perspective', *Annual World Bank Conference on Development Economics*, The World Bank (1996), p. 50.

7 Although these programmes had significant economic resources, their results were limited since Salinas in Mexico and Fujimori in Peru exerted personal control over them to direct many of the projects toward their own political objectives. For a critical approach about FONCADES and PRONASOL, see John Sheahan and Williams College, 'Effects of Liberalisation Programs on Poverty and Inequality: Chile, Mexico and Peru', *Latin American Research Review*, 32:3 (1997), p. 28.

8 For an explanation see United Nation, *The Global Compact: What It Is (2001)*. To be found at http://www.unglobalcompact.org/un/gc/unweb.nsf/content/whatitis. For a critical approach see United Nations, Global Policy Forum: *Let's Talk Business (2000)*. To be found at http://www.globalpolicy.org/reform/2000/1024gc.

9 For a discussion See Richard Higgott "Contested Globalisation: The Changing Context and Normative Challenges", *Review of International Studies*, 26 (2000) p. 153.

3 Country case studies, economic liberalisation implementation, and short-run results

The cases of Mexico, Brazil, Chile, and Uruguay are particularly interesting because they represent most of the liberalisation models in Latin America, and because they allow us to compare four different strategies of economic openness and four different forms of social inclusion during the mid-1980 and late 1990s, as well as their inherent results for income distribution, poverty, and the growth of the economy.

Mexico undertook a rapid economic liberalisation on the basis of neo-liberal orthodoxy; in addition, this course of action was conducted through a delegative democracy (DD). Therefore, Mexico provides important elements for evaluating the standard neoclassical theory, the original neoliberal model and their effects on income distribution, poverty, and growth.

Brazil introduced the neoliberal economic prescription and added some sociopolitical norms addressed in the Post-Washington Consensus (PWC), but the must outstanding feature of the Brazilian approach is the resistance the country showed at different times to abandon protectionist policies advocated in the ISI model; consequently, Brazil features traits to analyse a case of failure to perform sustained trade openness.

During the 1990s Chile adopted some regulations of capital flows without reject-ing economic liberalisation. In addition, this country adopted a broader notion of good governance and incorporated civil society in a top-down sense into policy-making. As a result, Chile provides some element for assessing if the prescription advocated by the PWC can improve income distribution and reduce poverty.

Uruguay enjoys a political system, which effectively aggregates major social demands; moreover, its social security system is perhaps the most con-solidated of the region. On the other hand, Uruguay remained a relatively closed economy during the 1980s and 1990s, and it was reluctant to conduct a major privatisation process. Hence, Uruguay provides interesting elements for evaluating whether a country can foster growth with equity under solid sociopolitical conditions and resistance to globalisation.

Mexico

The 1982 crisis signalled a period of severe economic contraction and adjustment for Mexico. In addition, IMF conditionality accounted for greater economic liberalisation during the late 1980s. However, the strong influence that technocratic groups and epistemic communities exerted on the federal government was crucial for the rapid implementation of the new economic model. In 1986, the government applied for membership of the General Agreement on Tariffs and Trade (GATT), and in 1987 it decided to pursue a unilateral tariff reduction and eliminate import permits (Heath 1998, 179). In addition, structural reforms included fiscal adjustment, privatisation, financial liberalisation, and the adoption of a fixed rule exchange rate as a cornerstone for preventing inflation. Moreover, minimum wages were not allowed to increase beyond the target rate of inflation.

These efforts were successful in lowering inflation. On the other hand, Alarcón and McKinley (1998, 139) stress that 'economic liberalisation combined with an overvalued exchange rate led to a rapid increase in imports and a sharp drop in production of importable for the domestic market, as well as a slowing in the growth of exports'. Furthermore, the government maintained a policy of high interest rates in order to attract capital inflows to finance the large current account deficit, but this policy inhibited domestic productivity investment by raising the cost of credit. The period 1989–1993 was characterised by an expansion of capital inflows on a broad scale. By 1993 the inflow of capital had risen to US$ 33.3 billion and portfolio investment led the surge with 87 per cent of the total flow (Instituto Nacional de Estadística Geográfica e Informática 2002), which made capital inflows extremely volatile rather than financing the long-term productive investment.

The enactment of the North America Free Trade Agreement (NAFTA) in January 1994 was a key element of the Mexican neoliberal economic policy. It generalised the US liberal rules to Mexico, especially in terms of foreign investment. Both market-oriented reforms and NAFTA negotiations included business elites in the decision-making process; however, other sectors of civil society were not included in policymaking. Economic liberalisation in Mexico was a product of a hegemonic political party and powerful presidentialism. In this concern, Cook outlines that Mexico's authoritarian political system of this epoch limited the ability of domestic political opponents to influence the political and economic process via elections or other domestic institutional means (Cook 1997, 521). The old political system was consistent with a DD or perhaps was more authoritarian; in 2000 it began the political alternation when the ruling party lost the presidential election after 70 years in power, but the current political system continues to be a DD. Over the 1990s, the tremendous gap that existed between civil society and the political system, the urgent need for a true democratic political reform, growing inequality, and economic deterioration increased civil society movements and social resistance. The uprising in the southern state of Chiapas in January 1994 symbolised the major opposition to neoliberal reforms and catalysed a national movement for broader political reform.

Macroeconomic mismanagement, economic volatility, and political instability caused adverse consequences, especially massive outflows of capital that culminated in the financial crisis of 1994–1995. The rapid economic liberalisation and the subsequent economic collapse resulted in economic stagnation, modest job creation, real wages decline, and growing inequality and poverty (see Table 2.1). Mexico is an illustrative case that reflects incompatibility between capital accumulation and wealth under the logic of neoliberalism and authoritarian DD. Nevertheless, Mexico is also an illustrative case in which there is some room for the liberal assertion, which contends that failure to develop is ascribed to macroeconomic mismanagement, improper government policies, and political and social obstacles.

After the 1994–1995 crisis Mexico undertook significant electoral reforms, decontrolled interest rates, and liberalised the exchange rate. In such circumstances Mexico practically adopted the full version of the Washington Consensus (WC). As a result, the country eliminated some macroeconomic inefficiency, and reached more political stability. Nevertheless, the neoliberal model has not evolved according to their theoretical foundations.

According to Alarcón and McKinley, most of the growth of manufactured exports was the result of intra-firm or intra-industry trade in a few sectors already highly internationalised, rather than any broad-based reorientation of domestic products toward exporting. They assert that the maquiladora industry was one of the few sectors enjoying rapid employment growth. However, since less than 2 per cent of their inputs are produced in Mexico, these enterprises had a weak multiplier effect on the rest of the country. Hence, their job creation effects throughout the economy were minimal. Furthermore, agriculture exports, which require labour-intensive activities, stagnated (Alarcón and McKinley 1998, 139–140). Thus, the pattern of trade specialisation does not reflect the country's endowment of abundant labour resources. Therefore, in the Mexican case adjustment to comparative advantages did not evolve as the neoliberal thesis suggests.

In this context, Pánuco and Székeley contend that Mexico increased trade flows, especially with the US, as a result of NAFTA, in goods that require medium-skilled labour following an intra-firm and intra-industry trade pattern. Moreover, from their point of view, trade liberalisation generated demand for the highest and relatively scarce skills used in certain services (e.g. financial). On the other hand, demand for unskilled labour in agriculture and the domestic industry stagnated. Hence, the lowest incomes did not respond to the factor price equalisation and inequality persists (Pánuco and Székeley 1996, 210–213). This fact undermines neoliberal foundations like the Heckscher-Ohlin theory, which stresses that the freeing of trade should shift factor demand in favour of unskilled labour and of agriculture in the LDCs and thereby improve the distribution of income.

After the 1994–1995 crisis, according to Mexican economic authorities, the value of the peso was in equilibrium as a result of the freely floating system. In contrast, entrepreneurs and some academics believed the peso was overvalued by between 20 and 30 per cent, meaning a disadvantage for Mexican exporters and a reduction in oil incomes (Jardón and Román 2001). An important fact is, by the late 1990s, the balance of trade became negative and the deficit expanded gradually.[1] To some extent, both FDI and foreign portfolio investment (FPI) favoured the overvaluation of the domestic currency. Although the exchange rate was market-determined, the neoliberal equation 'trade liberalisation plus capital inflows' tended to overvalue the peso, and therefore crowded out the production of competitive import substitutes, discouraged the development of new exports activities, and had regressive effects on income distribution. Consequently, the outcomes of both trade and capital account liberalisation in Mexico, under the logic of standard neoclassical theory, fit the arguments of the critical view, rather than the assumptions of the neoliberal precepts.

Tanski and French emphasise that in most cases export-oriented international corporations in Mexico were not open to linkages with local suppliers (e.g. the maquiladora industry). Moreover, foreign firms were often provided with attractive tax and export incentives and other fiscal subsidies (Tanski and French 2001, 678). It has been argued that under these circumstances, FDI does not crowd in domestic investment. In addition, downward pressure on corporation taxes decreases the scope for redistributive policies and increasingly moves the burden of taxation onto the less mobile factors, such as labour. Consequently, the scope of FDI for providing a positive contribution to economic growth, income distribution, and poverty in Mexico was limited to some extent. Thus, the benefits of FDI did not evolve according to the neoliberal assumptions.

The Mexican case reveals that privatisation can lead to capital concentration rather than better conditions for income redistribution and poverty reduction. In this view, Tanski and French show that between 1988 and 1995 the sales of the top 25 conglomerates as a percentage of GDP increased from 12 to 19 per cent. They claim that the privatisation process encouraged mergers and acquisitions in the manufacturing and in the banking sectors. In this process only the largest conglomerates and the wealthiest entrepreneurs were able to participate. As a result, between 1984 and 1999 the number of billionaires increased, but so did the percentage of the population living in poverty (Tanski and French 2001, 688). Furthermore, Tanski and French point out the largest companies in Mexico as the largest beneficiaries of trade liberalisation. During the 1990s, the top 25 firms (including transnational corporations) sharply increased their sales and export concentration ratios (ibid., 683). As a consequence, privatisation, trade liberalisation, and FDI of multinational corporations (MNCs) led to both capital and market concentration. This fact strengthens the critical position of the neoliberal prescription and undermines the basic liberal proposition of competitive markets.

Social programmes in Mexico, in this time, were aimed at dissipating destabilising sources of social tension, alleviating extreme poverty, and assisting victims of economic adjustment. These programmes were not aimed at long-term social investment or at dissipating the structural causes of poverty.[2]

Programa Nacional de Solidaridad (PRONASOL) has been one of the most ambitious transfer programmes not only in Mexico but in the whole of Latin America. Whitehead writes that it was intended to provide a permanent mechanism for delivery of public policy to those in greatest need. However, since it was heavily reliant on privatisation receipts and since it operated under conditions of fiscal stress, its resources were unstable and quite modest (1 per cent of GDP) (Whitehead 1996, 65). Hence, social programmes in Mexico operated within the logic of neoliberalism, that is, temporary relief without modifying structural causes of poverty. Since market forces did not encourage the efficient allocation of resources, social programmes were not enough to reverse the regressive impact on income distribution and to ameliorate the spread of poverty.

After the 1994–1995 crisis, Mexico adopted the full version of the WC, and the economy has been transformed into a more stable and quite sophisticated one. Nevertheless, high and sustained rates of economic growth, poverty alleviation, and income redistribution have not been achieved. Between 1986 and 1998 the annual average rate of growth was just 2.58 per cent.[3] In addition, Table 2.1 shows that both the proportion of urban households below the poverty line and the urban Gini coefficient in 1998 were substantially higher than they were in 1984. Moreover, the Economic Commission for Latin America and the Caribbean (ECLAC) illustrates that the proportion of total households below the poverty line hardly changed between 1989 and 1998, declining from 39 per cent to 38 per cent. ECLAC also notes that during the same period, the total Gini coefficient rose from 0.536 to 0.539 (ECLAC 2002, 44, 71).[4] Therefore, the original WC prescription seems to be idealistic and unfixable, as the Mexican experience revealed between the mid-1980s and early 2000s.

Brazil

In José Sarney's administration, between 1985 and 1990, the first civilian presidency in 21 years, the priority was to control hyperinflation; in this period there were no major changes in the trade sector. In the early 1990s, during the administration of Collor de Mello (1990–1992), the first government elected democratically after the military regime, the government launched a trade liberalisation programme; it was deemed to be the end of state intervention in favour of market-oriented policies and the beginning of the neoliberal era in Brazil. However, the programme was constrained, since the structure of import tariff rates resembled those used during the years of the ISI approach, as a select group of industries remained protected from imports (Arruda de Almeida 2004). The protected industries involved high technology, those with extensive backward linkages, and consumer goods with low comparative advantages in relation to East-Asian countries (Kume et al. 2001).

By 1992, the country had fallen into a hyperinflation crisis; in his presidency (1992–1994), Itamar Franco, the acting president after the impeachment of Collor de Mello, launched the Real Plan, whose main target was the reduction of inflation, with Fernando Henrique Cardoso as the minister of finance. The plan in 1994 involved three main strategies; they intensified the liberalisation model initiated in Collor de Melo's presidency. The first was a fiscal adjustment to encourage the reduction of the public deficit; it comprised, among other policies, public expenditure cuts, and the privatisation of state-owned enterprises, many of which had operated through a subsidy scheme, mainly in the sectors of telecommunications and electricity. The second strategy was the creation of a new currency, the 'real', and peg its value to the US dollar. The third strategy comprised the expansion of the trade liberalisation programme, through a package of tariff reduction, aimed at reducing domestic prices by increasing foreign competition and stabilising the currency; in addition, a tariff reduction agreement was signed in Mercosur (Arruda de Almeida 2004). Inflation decreased sharply in 1994, reaching two digits; the stabilisation of the economy boosted the domestic market, encouraged the flow of foreign investments, and eventually caused the appreciation of the domestic currency. This scenario contributed to increased fiscal income and improved the public account. The partial success of the Real Plan was a key factor in the election of Cardoso as president in 1994.

In 1995, during the Cardoso administration, which lasted until 2002, the domestic currency continued its appreciation, due to the surge of foreign investment, while inflation dropped to one digit. In this period, the government attempted to consolidate economic liberalisation policies. The appreciated exchange rate fostered industrial imports and stimulated industrial efficiency. On the other hand, the balance of payments started to deteriorate, mainly for two reasons: a sharp rise in consumption of imported goods, as a consequence of trade reforms and the strength of the domestic currency, and the Mexican crisis, which caused uncertainty and withdrawals of foreign investment in Latin America, including Brazil. These problems led the government to delay, and even reverse, the trade liberalisation programme. In fact, it was a retreat from trade reform, in which non-tariff barriers were reintroduced and tariff rates increased (Arruda de Almeida, *op. cit.*). Despite these efforts, the trade deficit was persistent during the Cardoso presidency. The economic crisis in México in 1995 and in Southeast Asia in 1997 urged the government to increase interest rates to retain foreign capital. Moreover, the debt increased rapidly in the period, as public and external deficit was balanced through national and international financing.

Regarding the liberalisation of the capital account, by 1997 Brazil had already provided the conditions to receive large flows of foreign capital. In this respect, Ferreira and Tullio (2002, 164) stress that the free access to international investments was an abuse, and argue that Brazil's government shared the view of the IMF and the US—it did not intend to exert controls on capital. Vernengo (2007, 85) shows that liberalisation of capital led to a sharp rise of internal debt in proportion to GDP in the 1990s; to some extent the debt was accumulated due to the increase in interest rates, as they were maintained at high levels in order to keep inflation under control. Despite the flow of investments and rising debt, the Brazilian economy was not as volatile as other economies in Latino America, and in episodes of either local or foreign crisis GDP did not drop sharply.

In terms of monetary policy, during the neoliberal era in the 1990s, Brazil adopted a fixed-peg regime, mainly to control inflation, as part of the Real Plan in 1994 and the process of economic and financial liberalisation, stated in the WC. The regime led to the appreciation of the currency and a greater current account deficit. The current account was controlled by lower rates of growth, reducing the demand for imports, and the flow of FDI.

The financial crises in the 1990s that started in Mexico, passed through Asia and Russia and ended in Argentina, demonstrated the fragility of fixed exchange rate regimes; after these events, policymakers in emerging markets tended to adopt more exchange rate flexibility. Brazil was not an exception; due to the unsustainability of the current account deficit, in 1999 the currency was devalued, and the country turned to an inflation-targeting regime. This change kept the commitment to the neoliberal agenda. The new regime was intended to build the credibility of the central bank and control inflation, without creating balance of payments problems, as those associated to the pegged regimes did; nevertheless, real interest rates remained high as in the pegged exchange period. Moreover, during both monetary regimes, inflation decreased, but unemployment rose and economic growth was low and unstable. That is to say, the government adopted orthodox policies that favoured stability over growth. Under these circumstances, the bargaining power of the labour force declined and caused a decrease in wages; as a result, the share of wages in total income dropped, resulting in changes in income distribution (Vernengo 2008).

In the Brazilian case, high interest rates, exchange rate appreciation, and low inflation benefited financial capital or rentiers, whereas they were barely affected by high unemployment rates. In contrast, the manufacturing sector and labour were more affected by the monetary regime (ibid., 101). Both policies, fixed-peg and inflation-targeting, incorporated high interest rates as a main instrument to keep the economy attractive to the flow of capital and to avoid balance of payments difficulties, but undermined growth, employment, and wages. This economic strategy was consistent with the WC prescription and the neoliberal agenda.

After the period of trade openness commencing in 1990, economic growth was volatile, showing negative rates in the early 1990s and low rates by the end of the decade. On average, the rate of economic growth between 1990 and 1999 was 1.88 per cent (World Bank 2020). Hence, economic growth was low compared to the expectations advocated in the orthodox prescription, and liberal policies were unable to re-establish higher growth rates. Policymakers thought the reasons for unstable and low growth were high interest rates, and the impact of external crisis, but mainly they blamed a large marginal propensity to import, boosted by imports liberalisation and currency appreciation. In this context, unstable growth was a reason to reverse free trade policies during Cardoso's mandate.

In the early years of civilian and democratic regimes, the civil society participation in a Gramscian sense, which emerged by the end of the 1970s as resistance against the military dictatorship, incorporated substantial opinion leadership in the decision-making process. In this respect, Leubolt (2014, 4) contends that this predominance led to the participation of various movements in the constitutional assembly in 1988. Leubolt also claims that the main social policy achievement of the new constitution was the establishment of minimum standards of 'social security', enabling the institutionalisation of a universalistic welfare regime, in which education, pension, healthcare, and social transfers were intended to be universally available to all citizens (ibid., 5).

President Cardoso not only embraced the social mandate of the 1988 Constitution, but also strengthened poverty reduction strategies. Furthermore, Leubolt argues that social policy was implemented democratically, as Cardoso established decentralised local councils, representing different policy sectors, and integrated them as respective decision-making bodies into the constitution. The reforms did not fit international trends toward a neoliberal programme; in contrast, the Brazilian Constitution and Cardoso's policies moved towards an equalitarian system (Leubolt 2014, 6).

According to Stuhlberger Wjuniski (2013, 155), with the arrival of democratic regimes and the reduction of political power of the elites, the social agenda and emphasis on education was intensified. He contends that the enactment of the third law in education in 1996 mandated compulsory and larger expenditure in both the federal government (18 per cent) and states and municipalities (25 per cent), and underlined allocation of more expenditure to the primary and secondary educational levels. These policies signalled the reversal of an unequal budget allocation in education, which lasted at least 25 years since the second law, and the return to the importance of social issues, as in Goulart's presidency.[5] In practice, investment increased in basic education, while access to public schools rose dramatically; as a result, illiteracy declined from 18 per cent in 1990 to 11.8 per cent in 2002 (Leubolt 2014, 7); but overall, government expenditure on education, as a percentage of GDP, fell during the presidency of Cardoso; according to World Bank figures, in 1995 the percentage was 4.6 and by 1999 it had fallen to 3.8 (World Bank 2020).

The social agenda in the Cardoso presidency additionally introduced programmes such as a monthly gas allowance for cooking purposes of R\$ 15 for the poor, *Bolsa Escola* and *Bolsa-Alimentação*, which were comparable to a family allowance, and provided a maximum amount of R\$ 45 a month for poor families, *Comunidade Solidária*, in which the state attempted to organise civil society's willingness to help, under the patronage of first lady Ruth Cardoso. The set of social policies aimed at poverty reduction via neoliberal economic policies in the Cardoso era is described as 'inclusive neoliberalism' (Leubolt, *op. cit.*, 10).

By the end of the ISI era's peak, and after a period of high economic growth, and increasing debt and inflation, the international banks refused to roll over the country's debt; and hence, the government undertook contractionary fiscal policy, which heavily affected the poor. As a matter of fact, the income of the poorest 50 per cent of the population, in relation to the national income, dropped from 17.4 per cent in 1960 to 12.6 per cent in 1980, whereas the share of the richest 10 per cent rose from 39.6 to 50.9. On these bases, Tranjan (2012, 146) argues that the poor, workers, and small producers carried the largest burden of Brazilian industrialisation.

The neoliberal policies in the 1990s, accompanied by high interest rates and slow growth, were unable to reverse the pattern of increasing inequality of income and bargaining power between the elites and the people, despite a more equitable law in education and the social policies in the Cardoso presidency; in fact, inequality increased after the implementation of liberal policies. In this respect, Vernengo (2008) illustrates that between 1990 and 2000, the share of wages, in relation to GDP, fell from 45.4 to 37.9 per cent, while the operational surplus's share, which includes profits, rents, and interest payments, increased from 32.5 to 40.6 per cent. This trend is corroborated in Table 2.1; it shows a rise in the Gini coefficient in Brazil between 1990 and 1996; moreover, ECLAC (2004, 76) also reports an increase in the Gini coefficients between 1990 and 1999 from 0.627 to 0.640.

On the other hand, as reported in Table 2.1, poverty decreased after reforms. The figures are in line with those from ECLAC (2004, 54), which show a drop in the household poverty indicator from 41.4 per cent in 1990 to 29.9 in 1999.

In the neoliberal era, high interest rates, imposed by the central bank, in line with anti-inflationary policies, led to a sharp increase in government payments for debt servicing, and eventually, to a substantial rise of public debt (Vernengo 2007, 86; Leubolt 2014, 8). The increase in interest payments and government debt servicing can foster crowding out of social spending; however, in the Brazilian case, it was different. The tax and contribution ratio as a percentage of GDP rose since 1996, after a period of volatility of this indicator; according to Leubolt (*op. cit.*, 7), the ratio rose from 25 per cent to 33 per cent between 1996 and 2002. This trend benefited per-capita social spending since it increased in the neoliberal regime, passing from less than US$ 800 in 1990 to US$ 936 in 2000 (ECLAC 2004, 36); the major benefit was concentrated in social assistance. The improvement in social expenditure, conducted mostly in the Cardoso presidency, kept Brazil in the third position in Latin America, with respect to this variable, only below Argentina and Uruguay and similar to Chile.

With the above in mind, poverty reduction in the 1990s was the result of higher and more efficient social expenditure, and the implementation of a set of inclusive social policies, but there were other important factors; it is worth noting price stability, the increase in minimum wages, and the industrialisation and urbanisation process. However, much of the improvements in social indicators are not related to the neoliberal era, and can be dated back to the ISI period. On the other hand, the persistence and even increase of income inequality can be explained by insufficient social expenditure and transfers, as well as more remuneration to capital, and the reduction of average wages and employment, that is to say, less bargaining power of the labour sector.

According to the review conducted above and the discussion in relevant literature (Arruda de Almeida 2004), the transition in Brazil from the ISI model to market-oriented policies illustrates how the country failed to implement sustained trade liberalisation programmes and the rigidity it had to abandon protectionist strategies. Brazil has been prone to face current account and public deficits, an overvalued domestic currency, and inflation; these difficulties forced the government to step back in the implementation of economic liberalisation polices or to restrict this set of policies, even during the 1990s, the decade in which neoliberal policies took root in the country. Moreover, epistemic communities that supported open markets were not as influential in Brazil as they were in countries like Mexico or Chile. In contrast, the industrial lobbying was influential to obtain benefits to specific industrial sectors, especially those fitting into the government's industrial strategy. Overall, the economic liberalisation in Brazil was subject to two main factors: the stabilisation of the macroeconomy and the reinforcement of a national industrial policy, and hence, it was not fully conducted.

The economic liberalisation process conducted in Brazil during the 1990s resembles the neoliberal economic prescription, incorporated in the WC, as it conducted trade and capital account liberalisation, privatisation of stated-owned enterprises, and encouraged the flow of investments. The model also moved towards public deficit reduction, an inflation-targeting monetary regime, and macroeconomic stabilisation. This model failed to achieve neoliberal distributional assumptions, as it benefited financial capital and undermined labour bargaining power.

On the other hand, the Brazilian case adopted some sociopolitical norms from the PWC, since there is evidence that it added civil society participation in the decision-making process, conducted basic forms of democratisation of social policies, and emphasised human capital formation; moreover, it established equalitarian social policies aimed at reducing poverty and addressing inequality. Both sociopolitical and economic norms in the Brazilian neoliberal era managed to reduce poverty, but failed to achieve more equalitarian conditions for the society. However, the most notorious characteristic of Brazilian neoliberalism is that it did not conduct deep and sustained market liberalisation; in contrast, the model tended to adopt strategic openness based on government industrial priorities and elites' lobbying.

Overall, the strategy of economic openness in Brazil showed some resistance to abandon the ISI approach, and it reversed trade openness policies in periods of macroeconomic instability.

Chile

Market-oriented policies in Chile were implemented by an authoritarian regime and by the ideological influence of a cohesive technocratic group after the military coup of 1973. Silva points out that the phase between 1975 and 1982 was a naïve stage of liberalisation within which Chile experimented with radical neoliberal policies with little regard for their effects on the domestic industry and labour. In addition, a narrow range of conglomerates was favoured on the basis of personal favours and clientelism. Corporate activity emphasised financial speculation over investment in production. After the implementation of radical neoliberal policies, the Chilean economy eventually faced an economic disaster in 1982/1983, when external conditions changed (Silva 1996, 304–307).

The 1982–1983 crisis was a turning point. Barton (1999, 68–69) underlines that between 1983 and 1989 the Pinochet regime adopted a pragmatic orthodoxy through improved financial controls and an export-led growth model that encouraged a greater diversification in the non-traditional sectors of the economy, such as forestry, fishery, and agriculture products, especially fresh fruit. Furthermore, tariffs came down in stages, and the cost of short-term investment rose. Silva (1996, 308–309) asserts that agriculture, mining, and manufactures received protection from unfair external competition. He explains how this set of pragmatic polices was negotiated between the regime, business peak associations, and landowners, especially in the new export industries. Silva holds that negotiations were carried out on the basis of technical criteria rather than personal favours, clientelism, or political threats. On the other hand, the regime created emergency employment and income transfer programmes during the early 1980s. Morley (1995, 68) holds that they possibly were big enough to reverse the regressive impact of recession and adjustment. This second stage of the military regime undertook prudential regulation, while emphasising poverty alleviation, but the neoliberal philosophy remained the main target.

Democratic regimes from 1990 have opted for the continuity of the pragmatic neoliberal economic model. The Chilean state has given priority to maintaining the confidence of business and simultaneously it has attempted to correct severe social inequalities by means of prudent social reforms.

Policy coalition between the state and business elites encouraged the diversification and expansion of non-traditional exports, and diversification of trading partners. The agenda of the negotiations included, on the one hand, assistance such as subsidies, tax credits, diplomatic advice, and training programmes; and on the other, policymaking in terms of government planning, processing of abundant raw materials, and strategic and staggered liberalisation, especially in trade and regional agreements. Under these circumstances, exports adjusted to comparative advantages; that is to say, natural resource-intensive activities that create jobs for unskilled labour.

Morley underlines that Chile undertook a complementary strategy of investing in education. This strategy dramatically increased enrolment ratios in secondary school and achieved almost complete coverage of both primary and secondary school-age children. In this way, an education- and export-driven strategy reduced supply and shifted factor demand in favour of unskilled labour (Morley 1995, 180–181).

Barrett (2001, 594) stresses that civilian governments 'remain committed to a neoliberal model that places a high priority on the maintenance of labour market flexibility as a key component of the economy's international competitiveness'. In order to counteract the negative effects of labour flexibility, the Aylwin government encouraged business to negotiate a modest labour reform that pursued rises in public pension, minimum wages, and job security. The reform was determined in tripartite negotiation between government, trade unions, and top business leaders. In this sense, Barton (1999, 73) claims that the labour reform was unable to counteract the flexibilisation of labour. Furthermore, Barrett (2001, 596) asserts that the primary effect of the reform was to consolidate the imbalance in capital–labour relations because since then, business presented a uniformly intransigent posture toward additional efforts aimed at strengthening the rights and income share of labour.

In 1990, the Aylwin administration proposed legislation for a tax on corporate earnings and increases in the value-added tax in order to fund spending on social programmes. The reform was consulted closely with encompassing business organisations and the parties in Congress. Most of the proposed changes targeted business sectors and the upper middle class and thereby had a redistributive effect. However, Weyland (1999, 74) points out that in subsequent public debates, the business sector showed its opposition to additional tax burdens.

The resources generated by the 1990 tax reform and high rates of economic growth allowed an enormous increase in social spending. Weyland emphasises that between 1989 and 1997 social expenditure more than doubled in real terms; priority sectors were public health and education. Moreover, he writes that the Aylwin and Frei regimes attempted to adopt inclusionary and consensual social programmes by supporting projects proposed by groups of microenterprises, the urban informal sector, and small rural producers through a demand-driven social fund (Fondo de Solidaridad e Inversión Social—FOSIS). The fund tried to enable poor people to achieve greater productivity in the market. By the same token, the strategy attempted to eliminate structural causes of poverty. However, he asserts that the fund is small in personnel, activities, and budget; moreover, it was unable to reach marginalised urban and rural sectors (ibid., 81–82). On the other hand, Chile's pension reform was a major policy innovation, which has been admired and copied in many other countries in the region—and the government contributes with substantial funds to the programme. Hence, social expenditure in terms of education, health, social programmes, and social security became an issue of major concern in the Chilean state.

Fernández (1996, 123) notes that the Chilean state reduced the degree of concentration in the stock market by increasing the number of individuals and enterprises participating in it. In effect, the privatisation of public enterprises was conducted with the aim of 'capitalismo popular'. As has been already commented on, this kind of policy is unlikely to encourage income redistribution, but at least is a strategy to dissipate further concentration.

After democratisation in 1990, policymakers viewed a huge infusion of capital, especially short-term capital flows, as a threat to both economic and political stability. As a result, they kept capital controls aimed at raising the cost of short-term investments. In this sense, Weyland (1999, 73) notes that these restrictions immunised Chile against the boom-and-boost cycle caused by highly volatile international capital investment. In fact, he holds that the fallout from Mexico's peso crisis was minor in Chile. Even the Asian Financial Crisis caused less damage in Chile than in other Latin America nations.

Scholars like Oxhorn (1999, 213) deem Chile's democratic regime among the most consolidated in Latin America. To some extent the Chilean institutionalised political party system, the strength of state institutions, and the aggregation of some groups of civil society mitigate the worst consequences of both polyarchy and the neoliberal model. Nevertheless, Chilean democracy suffers from serious limitations. As has already been commented on, the post-1989 democratic presidents retained much of the strongly presidentialist 1980 Constitution. In addition, the distribution of power between various groups within society was consistent with the kind of disproportional system that characterises a polyarchy. In this sense, elite business groups maintained privileged access to government, and the incorporation of labour groups and vulnerable sectors of society remained limited and was controlled from above by the state and business elite.

The Chilean model demonstrated potential in stimulating rapid export growth. As a matter of fact, from 1989 to 2001 Chile's exports expanded from US$ 8.08 billion to US$ 17.44 billion[6] and non-traditional exports grew 222 per cent between 1985 and 1997 (Grugel 1998, 226). Rapid export growth and political and macroeconomic stability contributed to achieving unprecedented economic growth. Between 1990 and 2000, the economy expanded at an annual average rate of 6.65 per cent.[7] Under these circumstances, the poverty rate declined impressively. Indeed, Table 2.1 shows that the proportion of urban households below the poverty line declined between 1990 and 1998. Furthermore, ECLAC (2002, 44) confirms this trend since it shows that the proportion of total households below the poverty line decreased from 33 per cent to 17 per cent between 1990 and 2000.

The version of the Chilean development model between the mid-1980s and early 2000s had a number of characteristics that were consistent with the PWC approach. Chile tried to consolidate the key norms of the WC since it did not reject emphasis on open markets and economic liberalisation and increase exports on the basis of comparative advantages. Simultaneously, the model highlighted the desirability of pragmatic and prudential regulation, especially in short-run investment in order to cope with financial turbulence. The Chilean strategy humanised economic liberalisation by adding more participation of civil society, human capital formation, and effective democratic regulation to the original economic norms of the neoliberal orthodoxy. However, these notions of good governance were implemented in a top-down adjustment controlled by state and business elites in order to facilitate and consolidate neoliberal strategies. These features of the Chilean model are compatible with the PWC rhetoric.

Although Chile adjusted exports to comparative advantages, it is not clear if this adjustment was due entirely to the operation of market forces and price mechanism. From this viewpoint, the state adopted developmental forms of organisation because it supported and coordinated investments, assisted the private sector, and targeted specific projects. Furthermore, corporate actors participated in policy coalitions. In addition, Collins and Lear notice that civilian governments prior to 1973 (during the time of the ISI model) placed preconditions for the boom in the agro-industry and forestry by enacting land reforms and cultivating areas that currently provide dramatic increases in yields (quoted in Richards 1997, 148). The Chilean experience undermined the neoliberal postulates and reveals that economic intervention of the state, corporative arrangements, and continuity of previous target-specific projects are necessary developmental strategies for boosting comparative advantages.

In 1974, about 80 per cent of Chilean exports were in copper (Gwynne 1999, 73). The export diversification strategy significantly reduced the single commodity export dependency; however, the country maintained large reliance on its natural resource base since it changed from mineral to marine, forestry, and cultivated resources. According to Barton (1999, 73), over 80 per cent of export earnings were derived from natural resource products. On the other hand, developmental strategies encouraged agro-industrial production and raw material processing, but they did not go further, fostering large-scale industrialisation. Broad reliance on natural resources created preconditions for economic vulnerability to international pricing, constrained market accessibility, and accelerated environmental degradation. In this respect, Richards (1997, 148–149) emphasises that the irrationality of forest management and the overexploitation of fishing resources in Chile are rapidly depleting native forest and stocks of fish, respectively. In such circumstances, sustained economic growth and stable exports cannot be guaranteed.

Although Chile encouraged poverty alleviation strategies, the canons of neoliberalism advanced the interest of capital and weakened the bargaining power of labour; moreover, vulnerable sectors were constrained in the policy-making process. Thus, the Chilean model seemed to accept capital accumulation, while income distribution played a secondary role, like in the PWC prescription. In this context, Oxhorn (1999, 210) claims that despite the dramatic drop in the poverty level and the unprecedented economic performance in terms of growth, there was no significant improvement in income distribution during the 1990s. Indeed, Table 2.1 shows slight regressive effects in the urban Gini coefficient between 1990 and 1998, whereas ECLAC (2002, 71) illustrates that the total Gini coefficient rose from 0.554 to 0.559 between 1990 and 2000. In short, the version of the PWC model applied in Chile had demonstrated potential by the early 2000s in reducing poverty and stimulating export growth, and achieved an unprecedented economic expansion. Nevertheless, the model had serious shortcomings for dissipating income inequality and did not form the basis for sustained economic growth.

Uruguay

Historically, Uruguay has enjoyed an institutionalised political party system with real ties to civil society, which effectively aggregates major social demands. Furthermore, its social security system is one of the oldest and most developed in the region and the percentage of public spending devoted to it (22.4 per cent of GDP in 1996)[8] is the largest in Latin America. Not surprisingly this country has been considered the continent's first welfare state and model democracy.[9]

Panizza explains that after the coup of 1973 the economic strategy was based on neoliberal/monetarist principles; the military regime suspended the Constitution, closed Congress, and banned all political and trade union activity. He emphasises that the economic collapse that swept the region in the early 1980s was instrumental in the fall of the military regime. The civilian regime was recognised for restoring democracy, human rights, and the constitutional order in 1985, but its economic policies came under attack. In this respect, Panizza writes that the centre-right government was unable to change radically the economic policies of the previous regime since it was constrained by external debt. By the same token, its priority was to gain the support of the IMF. In late 1985 an agreement was reached with the fund, which included the opening of the economy, the deregulation of financial markets, and commitments to reduce inflation and the public deficit (Panizza 1990, 166–174). In this context, Helwege (1995, 112, 114) underlines, despite this adjustment, that social expenditures did not tend to decrease and inequality fell between 1980 and 1993. This is because Uruguay succeeded in maintaining the sophistication of its social welfare institutions after the restoration of democracy.

Despite conditionality exerted by International Financial Institutions (IFIs), Uruguay emerged as a country highly resistant to neoliberal transformation. In this respect, Filgueira and Papadópulos point out that conditionalities imposed by international lending agencies led to public expenditure cuts as a means of reducing the fiscal deficit. However, associations of retirees and pensioners in Uruguay forged a policy coalition with diverse parts of all political parties and the trade union movement and systematically opposed attempts to reform social security. 'In 1987 this coalition blocked a proposal to reform the system inspired by recommendations of the World Bank. It also succeeded in establishing that no retirement benefit could be lower than the nationwide minimal wage by 1990.' Furthermore, in 1989, along with national elections the organisation of retired persons called for a plebiscite on a constitutional reform that would incorporate an automatic indexation of benefits. The reform was supported by 82 per cent of the voters (Filgueira and Papadópulos 1997, 365–366).

The labour movement, autonomous of the state and enterprises, historically has had high legitimacy in public opinion; moreover, it became part of a true party system, specially linked to the Left. Consequently, the labour movement enjoys substantial collective bargaining power in business–labour negotiations. Under these circumstances, Filgueira and Papadópulos assert that procedures such as hiring and dismissing people became more flexible; nevertheless, there were no significant changes in the provision of Uruguayan law involving labour protection, which are considered especially advanced (ibid., 368).

Filgueira and Papadópulos emphasise that minority parties play a significant role in the nomination of enterprise directors; furthermore, these directors are free to appoint functionaries based on technical criteria. Moreover, they assert that the management of public enterprises, conduced according to a logic of political distribution and technical and political co-participation, constituted the foundational matrix of public enterprises and allowed efficiency in them, which have been an engine of economic growth. Filgueira and Papadópulos also note that the military regime made no attempt to modify the property regime governing public enterprises. In addition, the Sanguinetti government failed even to achieve a parliamentary debate to transfer some healthy public enterprises to the private sector or to public–private partnerships as a result of union opposition and resistance from political parties. Furthermore, President Lacalle succeeded in passing the Law of Privatisation of Public Enterprises in Congress, but the Left faction of political parties and the union movement sought a referendum to overturn the key provisions of the law. In 1993, 70 per cent of the voters repealed the critical articles of the law, thus burying the privatisation project as a whole (ibid., 374–378).

According to Panizza, the country's traditional exports comprise beef, wool, hides, and some agricultural crops, whereas non-traditional exports (NTE) comprise shoes, leather goods, fish, rice, semi-precious stones, and some light consumer goods. They have a higher industrial content than the traditional ones without requiring substantial transformation of Uruguay's industry (Panizza 1990, 167). NTE did not register significant expansion. Between 1985 and 1998 manufactured exports as a percentage of total exports grew from 35.0 to 38.7 per cent. Furthermore, exports have declined since the ratio of exports as a percentage of GDP dropped from 26.8 to 19.8 per cent during the same period.[10] In addition, these statistics suggest that for such a small economy the country traditionally has been relatively closed. Although Uruguay has experienced the dismantling of the public sector and the growing predominance of the market, this transformation has been weak and tenuous, and exports are still led by public enterprises.

The easy access to plebiscite, the balance in labour–capital relations, the existence of referendums that favour the formation of extra-parliamentary coalitions, the institutional framework of the social security system that favours consolidation of new social actors, and the absence of a hegemonic political elite inhibit models of neoliberal democracies and exclusionary policymaking. Filgueira and Papadópulos claim that the absolute level of popular sector incorporation into the development model, the social security system based on equal distribution rather than individual capitalisation, and the clientelist system that functions less as a mechanism of domination and more as an instrument of popular incorporation tend to generate strategies of aggregation rather than atomisation and create structural bases for potential alliance among all system beneficiaries. Hence, Uruguay's social matrix generates high resistance to change.

Despite resistance to economic liberalisation and private investment, since the mid-1980s and through the 1990s the aftermath of the Uruguayan's model has been positive. Table 2.1 illustrates that in this period the proportion of urban households below the poverty line and the urban Gini coefficient declined substantially; in 1997 they were the lowest in the region. In addition, ECLAC shows that the total Gini coefficient decreased from 0.492 to 0.440 between 1990 and 1999 (ECLAC 2002, 71). Moreover, between 1985 and 1998 the country also achieved relatively high economic growth rates: an annual average of 4.01 per cent.[11]

On the other hand, between 1999 and 2002 Uruguay faced up to a drastic fall in the economy and suffered bank panics, a financial crisis, and devaluation of the domestic currency, which eventually triggered social protests (*El Mundo al Revés* 2002). According to the United Nations Development Programme, the economic decline of those years raised poverty to 22 per cent of the population (quoted in *loc. cit.*). This economic crisis emerged as a result of the Brazilian crisis in 1998 and worsened with the Argentinean financial collapse in December 2001. Nevertheless, increasing public and trade deficits, increasing external debt, and a weak financial and banking system that required further private investment both foreign and domestic were also determinant factors in the crisis (*loc. cit.*).

From a PWC perspective, civil society participation, social and human capital formation, and effective democratic regulation legitimise and favour the implementation of market-oriented reforms, but these notions of good governance need to be implemented in a top-down adjustment from the bottom up. The Uruguayan case reveals that when social and human capital formation based on equal distribution and when real participatory democracy that effectively aggregates legitimate social demands are implemented in a bottom-up sense, neoliberal policies are inhibited rather than favoured, and effective income redistribution can be achieved. However, the Uruguayan democratic system showed serious limitations in the long run.

The strategies of aggregation function as a clientelist system that incorporates a large proportion of the population; thus, they tend to generate high resistance to change. This fact inhibits economic liberalisation, which was a determining cause of the economic difficulties in Uruguay between 1999 and 2002. Consequently, this country, up to the early 2000s, reveals that incorporation from below is essential for income redistribution, but it also illustrates that this kind of democratic system needs to be improved. In other words, clientelist forms of organisation need to be replaced by consensus, negotiation, and greater consciousness among civil society, political parties, and the government so as to allow economic liberalisation to be compatible with income distribution.

After the policy reform and the implementation of the economic liberalisation agenda in Latin America during the 1980s and 1990s, some countries in the region transitioned to central planning and statist regimes, notably Venezuela and Bolivia. As for the four countries analysed in this book, they have kept orthodox and neoliberal economic policies over the last two decades, with no significant changes regarding the economic models they originally built, despite the fact they have alternated between Right and Left governments. Under these circumstances, Mexico, Brazil, Chile, and Uruguay provide relevant case studies to analyse the long-term performance of economic liberalisation under different social policies and democratic models. In the following chapter, we explore the policy agenda in these countries over the last two decades, as well as the performance of key variables along the whole period of analysis.

Notes

1 The balance of trade as a percentage of GDP moved from –1.8 per cent to –4.6 per cent between 1997 and 2000. Source: Authors' computation with information from Banco de Mexico, *Informacion Financiera* (Mexico City 2001). Available at: http://www.banxico.org.mx/eInfoFinanciera.

2 For a brief description of transfers programmes in Mexico, see Samuel A. Morley, *Poverty and Inequality in Latin America: The Impact of Adjustment and Recovery in the 1980s.* (Baltimore: The Johns Hopkins University Press, 1995), pp. 74–75.

3 Source: Authors' computation with information from World Bank, *World Development Indicators,* CD-ROM (Washington, DC, 2001a).

4 For a discussion on the affectations of economic liberalisation in income distribution, see Gerardo Angeles-Castro (2007) Factors Driving Changes in Income Distribution in Post-Reform Mexico, University of Kent, Department of Economics, Discussion Paper, 07/06.

5 The left wing Goulart government (1961–1964) placed more emphasis on social issue than his predecessors; in fact, it was during this time that the first law in education was approved, generating increase in expenditure in all educational levels and a positive impact on school enrolment rates. Economic and political instability and the fear of socialism led to a military regime in 1964. The second law in education did not enforce the federal government to spend a specific budget requirement; in contrast, it could spend the sum it wanted in education; furthermore, it withdrew the secondary education as a public good and was aimed at utilising loans for students. It also targeted large investments in higher education to form skilled labour needed for growth. This set of policies resulted in inequality between levels of education and declining secondary school quality, stimulating basic education for the poor and higher education for the rich, and leading to an increasing gap between economic classes (Stuhlberger 2013, 151–153).

6 Source: Central Bank of Chile, *Base de Datos Economicos* (Santiago de Chile, 2002). Available in www.bcentral.cl/indicadores/excel/balanza_comercial.xls

7 Source: Authors' computation with information from Central Bank of Chile, op. cit.

8 Source: International Labour Organization, *World Labour Report 2000; Income Security and Social Protection in a Changing World* (Geneva: International Labour Office, 2000), p. 314.

9 See, for example, R. Kaztman, F. Filgueira, and M. Furtado, 'New challenges for equity in Uruguay', *CEPAL Review*, 72 (2000), pp. 79–98.
10 Source: World Bank, *World Development Indicators*, CD-ROM (Washington, DC, 2001b).
11 Source: Authors' computation with information from World Bank *op. cit.*

4 Long-run evolution of equity and growth

Now that we have discussed the implementation of economic liberalisation and the results during the 1990s and early 2000s, we now present a discussion on the economic and social spectrum in the four countries over the last two decades or so and the evolution of three main variables—economic growth, poverty, and income distribution—with a long-term perspective. The discussion is complemented by an analysis of the evolution of relevant variables for the four country case studies using observations made since the mid-1980s, the period in which liberalisation started or was consolidated in several Latin American regions, to recent years, so as to have a long-term picture of the social and economic performance in the four countries.

Mexico

In the last two decades, Mexico has continued the consolidation of policies and reforms that prioritise the liberation of markets and favour international capital. At the beginning of the millennium, the sale of the main private banks to foreign corporations was carried out; even this sale was prioritised over the merger of two of the main banks when they were still owned by national investors. In this scenario, national capitalism was also favoured because there were sales processes in which the payment of taxes was exempted or a part of them was condoned.

The consolidation of neoliberalism in Mexico and the 'internationalisation' of capital not only seek to eliminate obstacles to the operation of markets and build institutions that strengthen the markets, but can also be seen as a set of policies to strengthen the relationship between the state and the global accumulation of capital (Muñoz-Martínez 2008).

The accelerated 'modernisation' of the economic system in the twenty-first century imposed the need for state reform, although this has allowed the transition to political alternation,[1] and has been conducted as a controlled reform, directed from above and seeking to avoid the collapse of the regime, but not a thorough democratisation (Hernández-Rodríguez 2015). As a result, a regime of presidentialism and partidocracy prevails, dominated by centre-right and humanistic political institutes up to 2018; just in this year the leftist

MORENA party won the presidential election, but this recent political alternation has not involved changes either in the presidentialist system or in the hegemony of political institutions. Moreover, the political and business elite continues to be privileged in the decision-making process, and the equitable distribution of income and social equality is limited. The leftist government has removed support and budget that was allocated for civil society organisations in previous governments, and has taken advantage of its majority in Congress to undermine the autonomy of agencies such as the National Commission of Human Rights and the Federal Institute of Telecommunications, among others. Previous regimes' achievements, comprising partial civil society participation, the creation of autonomous agencies, and some balance between the executive, legislative, and judicial powers, have been diminished in the new leftist regime. Under these circumstances, the division of powers has been weakened and there is evidence of a return to a highly presidential regime.

In terms of wage inequality and income distribution, it was expected that economic liberalisation, and in particular Mexico's entry to NAFTA, would increase the demand for the abundant factor—unskilled labour—and therefore, there would be an increase in real terms of wages and a redistribution of income, according to standard neoclassical theory. However, although between 1980 and 2008 productivity per worker increased by 92 per cent, the institutionally determined minimum wage lost two thirds of its purchasing power and the average unskilled real wage decreased by 22 per cent in the same period; in contrast, the average skilled real wage increased 8 per cent (López et al. 2012), which caused persistent wage inequality. In general, and up to the present year, real wages have stagnated, economic growth has been low, no more than 2.5 per cent in average since 2000, and in 2019 the country faced increasing unemployment and entered economic recession. As a result, poverty and income inequality remain high.

Overall and after more than 20 years, the promises expected from NAFTA were not fulfilled; on the one hand, greater integration between the United States and Mexico was generated, and the country became a consolidated exporter of manufactures; on the other hand, both countries have not converged on GDP per capita, unemployment problems in Mexico have not been resolved, migration to the United States continues, and manufacturing employment grew marginally (Blecker 2015). Over the last few years the problems stressed by Blecker persist. These points reflect that some of the neoclassical postulates in which the expectations of NAFTA were based were not achieved in the short term and remain unattainable in the long term.

The openness of the Mexican economy has resulted in a more competitive country in international markets, but also in more dependence on foreign demand and especially on the US economy. Eventually, the country has become more exposed to changes in foreign markets and international financial volatility. In fact, in 2001 the country was seriously affected by the bursting of the technology firms' bubble, as the slowdown in the US growth started a recession, in which the Mexican GDP declined by 2 per cent. Later on, the global economic crisis of 2008, whose epicentre was in the US, affected the Mexican economy more than it affected most other Latin American economies, and the GDP in the country fell by 6 per cent in 2009 (Carrera-Troyano and Domínguez-Martín 2017). These affectations occurred in Mexico despite the fact that their macroeconomic fundamentals were strong and stable before the economic difficulties erupted in both episodes. It is also interesting to note that the rise in the price of commodities and food, which took place on a global scale over the last decade, has had a greater impact on the cost of living and economic volatility in Mexico, whose market is more open and exposed to international prices.

The competition of emerging countries aspiring to increase their share of the US market has exposed Mexican exports to more volatility. Furthermore, Mexican integration with, and dependence on, the North American market has constrained trade diversification and economic integration with other relevant economic regions in the world. In this sense, Mexico has not benefited from China's economic growth and its increasing role in the world economy, as other Latin American countries have done, because the country has not consolidated its export to that Asian economy. In contrast, China has competed against Mexico to place its products in the US market, causing a drop in manufacturing exports (Carrera-Troyano and Domínguez-Martín 2017). The economic openness model used by Mexico since the mid-1980s has, therefore, exposed the country to financial volatility, international competition in the US market, and price instability, which eventually had a direct impact on poverty growth and on economic volatility and has led the economy to perform poorly.

In 2019 NAFTA was revised and emerged as the USMCA (United States–Mexico–Canada Agreement); it is argued that the new deal creates more balanced and reciprocal North American Trade. Nevertheless, for Mexico it does not solve problems of trade concentration and market instability, and does not provide growth incentives. In fact, Mexico accepted US conditionality in negotiation rounds, which were signalled by US threats on migration policy and trade regulations.

The increasing flow of foreign direct investment and trade volume are expected to create the conditions to reduce the informal economy, tackle corruption, and improve wages, based on the principle of comparative advantages and liberal theory. However, the results show a different picture; in this respect, Instituto Nacional de Estadística Geográfica e Informática (2020) reports that the informal economy in Mexico remains relatively high (with a negligible drop between 2001 and 2016), as it passed from 23.6 to 22.5 per cent of GDP in the period; furthermore, the CONASAMI (2020) indicates that the minimum wage increased between 2016 and 2019 in real terms, but historically it has lost 63.7 per cent of its value since 1982, the year of the debt crisis, up to 2019. It should be added that the political rights indicator, a proxy of the status of democracy in a country, has a scale of 1 to 7 (1 being the best position), and Mexico, with a value of 3 and with no improvements between 1984 to 2020, is classified as partially free (Freedom House 2020).

Due to the liberalisation process, besides the formalisation of the economy, the increase of the manufacturing sector was also expected, and the combination of both factors would eventually increase tax revenue. Although the manufacturing sector has presented a sharp increase, the informal sector is still a substantial proportion of the economy, as commented before; this limitation, besides others, has kept tax revenue at low levels. Between 2003 and 2018 the tax revenue increased from 19.87 to 22.65 as a percentage of GDP (OECD 2020a), the expansion is marginal and the percentage still remains low, compared to other Latin American and Organisation for Economic Co-operation and Development (OECD) economies.

During the last three decades, Mexico has achieved political alternation and has transitioned between centre-right, humanistic, and leftist regimes. Despite government changes, the Mexican model has kept a highly liberalised economy; the social programmes, although diverse, have been insufficient to further tackle poverty and inequality, and they remain clientelist.

All these facts, during the era of economic liberalisation in Mexico, are associated with persistent income inequality and poverty, and slow growth of GDP and GDP per capita.

Figure 4.1 and Figure 4.2 show GDP growth and GDP per capita (in constant 2010 US$) between 1985 and 2018, respectively. In the former we can see that economic growth has been volatile, with sharp drops in 1986, 1995, 2001, and 2009; on average annual GDP growth in the period was 2.45 per cent, the slowest of the four studied countries; and in the latter we can see that GDP per capita increased from US$ 7,872 to US$ 10,403 in the period, that is 32 per cent in real terms in 33 years, which has also been the slowest performance of the four country cases.

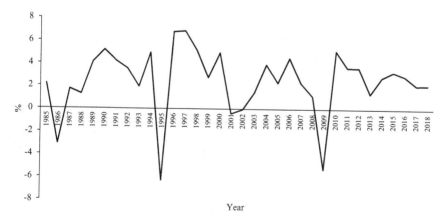

Figure 4.1 GDP growth, annual percentage for Mexico
Source: World Bank (2020)

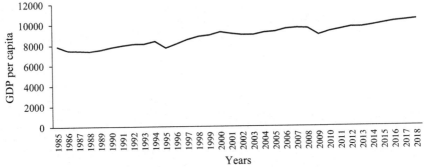

Figure 4.2 GDP per capita for Mexico, in constant 2010 US$
Source: World Bank (2020)

The poverty headcount ratio at US$ 5.50 a day (2011 PPP) as a percentage of population is presented in Figure 4.3, for the period 1989–2016. We use the same indicator for Brazil, Chile, and Uruguay because it is comparable among the four countries, and not the poverty ratio at national poverty line, because it changes from country to country. The indicator has declined from 40.1 to 25.7 per cent in the period, about 15 percentage points. This reduction was mainly achieved between 2000 and 2012, the years of the two humanistic governments, and took place after a rebound as a consequence of the internal financial crisis of 1994–1995. Despite the drop, the population living below this poverty line is still high and the largest from the four countries.

In 27 years, between 1989 and 2016, the Gini coefficient fell by 6 points, from 54.3 to 48.3, as presented in Figure 4.4. There has been a marginal improvement in terms of income distribution in Mexico, but the drop of the indicator has been slow and inequality is still high; only Brazil surpasses the inequality of Mexico of the four countries studied.

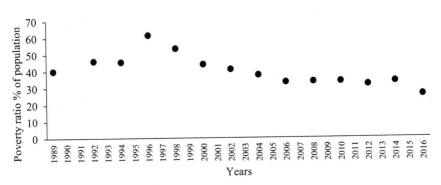

Figure 4.3 Poverty headcount ratio, US$ 5.50 a day (2011 PPP), as a percentage of the
population, Mexico
Source: World Bank (2020)

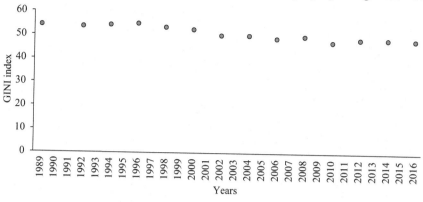

Figure 4.4 Gini index in Mexico (World Bank estimates)
Source: World Bank (2020)

To sum up, Mexico has been a liberal economy since the mid-1980s, and more open to markets than most Latin American countries; political rights and participatory democracy have not been consolidated, and there is an unbalance of power between capital and labour. In the humanistic governments, there were efforts to consolidate autonomous institutions and the participation of civil society organisations in order to reduce presidentialism, but the hegemony of the executive power is returning with the new leftist government. Hence, the Mexican model continue to be attached to the basic economic rules of the WC approach, regardless of the kind of regime. Moreover, the economic and sociopolitical model, during the period of economic liberalisation, is associated with a slow expansion of GDP and GDP per capita, and high and persistent poverty and inequality.

Brazil

In the 1990s the neoliberal reforms and the contribution of social policies led to the promotion of 'inclusive liberalism'. From the mid-2000s onwards, policies began to shift in the direction of 'developmental welfare', combining active state interventionism in economic and social policies with targeted cash transfers (Leubolt 2014, 5). Luiz Inácio Lula da Silva emerged from the leftist Labour Party (PT) and governed between 2003 and 2010, supported by two platforms: demands for a socialist democracy, and the interest of the organised (formal) working class (Arestis and Saad-Filho 2007, 1).

The next president was Dilma Rousseff, who mainly continued Lula's agenda: she governed Brazil between 2011 and 2016, after which she was impeached. During the Cardoso administration and the PT's regimes, the economic strategy did not change significantly, since orthodox liberal policies continued and the monetary policy primarily targeted inflation. In fact, in Lula's first administration Cardoso's fiscal and monetary policies were intensified, while conservative economic and social policies were adopted throughout the period (Arestis and Saad-Filho, *op. cit.*, 2). The PT economic model became, hence, a state-driven capitalist development.

The political economy of the PT presidencies is also known as neo-developmentalism; its challenge was to reconcile positive aspects of neoliberalism, such as commitment to currency stability, fiscal austerity, international competitiveness, and promotion of international capital, with positive aspects of the old developmentalism, such as commitment to economic growth, industrialisation, a regulatory state, and social sensitivity (Barbosa dos Santos 2019, 218). It is also worth noting that the PT adopted the trade openness strategy used by previous governments, based on government industrial priorities and elites' lobbying, and therefore market liberalisation kept some forms of restriction.

Leubolt (*op. cit.*, 11–12) points out that Lula's main social target was the eradication of hunger, and the corresponding strategy focused on the expansion and improvement of the conditional cash transfer programme, in which the grants where conditioned to medical attendance of the family and school attendance of the children. He also indicates that in 2001 the Cardoso government introduced the first conditional cash transfer programmes on a national scale, while Lula's administration unified the programs into *Bolsa Família* and extended its coverage and the amount transferred. The programme reached over 13 million families in 2012 and turned into an electoral platform for the PT; the allocation was conducted via state-owned banks so as to avoid conventional clientelism. Moreover, Leubolt stresses the concern in the literature for the repercussions of *Bolsa Família*, as, on the one hand, it was considered a programme that caused perverse disincentives to searching for employment on the labour market, and on the other hand, it encouraged the formalisation of labour relations of recipients—in other words, some recipients and former recipients found formal jobs. It might be because family members improved their skills and health conditions. He argues that, in general, *Bolsa Família* has been considered a successful programme for poverty reduction.

In the Lula administration, the economy grew 4.08 per cent per year, on average; this expansion was mainly the result of the stabilisation of the economy (a consequence of the Cardoso presidency), the rise in international commodity prices, and accelerated Chinese growth. According to Leboult, the positive economic conditions allowed for the rise in social spending by the federal government, as it moved from 13.82 to 15.80 as a percentage of GDP between 2005 and 2009. The additional social spending benefited different policies; in this respect, the universal provision of education was strengthened, especially in higher education and disadvantaged segments; public investment also increased in infrastructure (sewage and housing), employment, and pensions, besides social assistance and health. Despite the increasing public investment, the Lula administration kept a primary surplus above 2.7 per cent of GDP in every year, except in 2009, while payments to debt servicing gradually decreased; however, the final deficit remained above 2.5 per cent for most of the period (Leboult, *op. cit.*, 19–22).

This fact raised concern about the sustainability of the neo-developmentalism model in the PT regime by the end of Lula's presidency; nevertheless, at the time, the model had already achieved a recovery in wages, improvements in the distribution of income, reduction of poverty, and lower unemployment.

The foreign policy of Brazil in the Lula government was aimed at vindicating the role of the country as a regional leader and replacing the historical leadership of the United Sates in the subcontinent by promoting South American integration; an important action in this respect was the founding of the Union of South American Nations (UNASUR) in 2008. The process came at a time when leftist political leaders reached the presidency in most South American nations (only Colombia and Peru leaned to the right) (Barbosa dos Santos 2019, 217); this fact was expected to facilitate the dissemination of Brazilian foreign policy ideology, known as post-neoliberal regionalism. The policy also comprised diversification of strategic partnership with Asian and African countries and friendly relations with developed economies.

The protagonist factor supporting the regional economic policy was the strategy to internationalise large Brazilian corporations, carried out through entrepreneurial diplomacy and the credit policy adopted by the Brazilian Development Bank (BNDES). The bank offered a credit line to foster the international expansion of corporations that exported Brazilian goods and services and were headquartered in the country. The policy benefited concentrated and oligopolised sectors of the economy, in the fields of construction, energy and oil, and commodities, comprising products such as soybeans, ethanol, minerals, meat, and paper and cellulose. In some cases, these sectors were associated with business chains dominated by transnational corporations. The BNDES contributed to boost capital concentration; by 2010, 700 mergers and acquisitions had been conducted, involving Brazilian firms and South American counterparts. The international expansion emphasised civil construction; in this sense, BNDES expanded loans to Brazilian building contractors abroad. The countries in which mergers and acquisitions and construction projects focused were Argentina, Bolivia, Chile, Paraguay, Peru, and Venezuela, and Cuba and the Dominican Republic in the Caribbean, among others. The PT's international strategy pursued the political autonomy of the region under Brazilian leadership, in which the internationalisation of Brazilian corporations would become the basis to consolidate regional influence, as part of a process to place Brazil on the road to being a global player (Barbosa dos Santos 2019, 220–222).

The internationalisation of Brazil concentrated on countries with ideological affinities and close political ties; outside the subcontinent and the Caribbean economic and commercial connections were less relevant. Hence, Brazil attempted to become a regional capitalist leader, with economic, political, and ideological domination on the subcontinent, in the form of post-neoliberal regionalism. That is to say, the international political economy of

Brazil resembled the dominant capitalist practices that were criticised by the theorists of structuralist and dependency theories, and confronted by Latin American governments and countries for many years.

The BNDES's projects were involved in several social and environmental problems, leading to popular opposition. Moreover, the bank's function raised concern, as it was deemed to be a supporter of oligopolies and corporations and not an entity with social benefits. Barbosa dos Santos (2019, 224) illustrates the controversial roles of firms that benefited from BNDES loans; the cases include a sugar mill accused of keeping workers in precarious conditions, the meat packer denounced for keeping cattle in areas illegally deforested, and a long-term strike in a nickel company. In particular, the construction of hydroelectric plants in several locations caused workers to rebel, had a large social and environmental impact, uncertain economic viability, indigenous movements, and social protests, not only in Brazil, but also in countries such as Bolivia and Peru. The foreign policy was also associated with corruption, especially in the civil construction sector, and inappropriate allocation of funds, as the resources benefited foreign corporations in some cases. Barbosa dos Santos (*op. cit.*, 225) argues that overall there is no consistent evidence showing that the services provided by BNDES stimulated output growth.

Dilma Rousseff took office in 2011 and her presidency lasted until 2016. She did not emphasise the international agenda nor regional integration. At the time, the economy of Brazil showed signs of deterioration due to lower economic growth in China, and a commodity price reduction in international markets. Moreover, the burden of social spending and overall increases in public expenditure caused a rise of per-capita debt and sustained public deficit, which forced the economy to slow. By 2015 the economy had fallen into recession and presented negative growth by more than 3 per cent for two years (see Figure 4.5). Despite the reduction in poverty and inequality, the poor sectors marginally benefited from the economic policy, whereas large

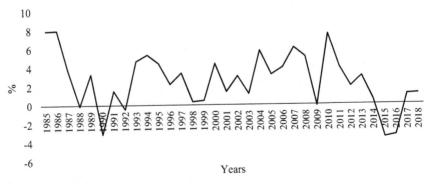

Figure 4.5 GDP growth, annual percentage for Brazil
Source: World Bank (2020)

firms and corporations obtained substantial gains; this fact raised social discontent. The corruption scandals involved several PT projects, and questions emerged in relation to the efficiency of multinational firms. The combination of economic crisis, corruption, and social discontent resulted in a loss of PT popularity and political gains for the right.

Following the social, political, and economic difficulties faced by the Brazilian government, in April 2016 Congress voted to impeach president Dilma Rousseff, and a few month latter the senate confirmed the decision. Avritzer (2017, 349–350) states that the governability crisis has several dimensions: the collapse of the coalition presidential system based on the exchange of public positions for support in Congress led to generalised corruption and a loss of credibility of the political system; a change in economic policy in May 2012, which implied moving away from an alliance with the financial markets and trying to establish a new alliance with the industrialists—the change resulted in adverse reaction by the financial markets and the whole economic elite; the absence of media regulation, allowing ownership concentration, besides the position of the main media groups that adopted an anti-PT stand, expressing negative reports in almost all the aspects of the economy. These dimensions led to the defeat of the neo-developmentalism and post-neoliberal regionalism coalition and the surge of a new economic and political coalition against the PT. However, the new coalition was unable to overcome the political, social, and economic difficulties, in which the country was immersed.

Michel Temer took office in August 2016 after the impeachment of Dilma Rousseff and served until December 2018, when Rousseff's second presidential period had been expected to end. His presidency was characterised by low economic growth (Figure 4.5) and a marginal increase in poverty and inequality (see Figure 4.7 and Figure 4.8) as a repercussion of the economic crisis started in 2013. During his presidency, he was accused of corruption, including obstruction of justice, accepting bribes, and organised crime. The combination of corruption and economic and social deterioration in the Temer administration caused massive protests, social discontent, and a dramatic loss of his popularity; despite this fact, he refused to resign, though he did not run in the following election.

The right-wing Bolsonaro took office in 2019, after a long period of erosion of the left and the collapse of its public policy. He inherited a country in precarious conditions, with high rates of unemployment and a large informal market—and the largest figures in the word for homicides per 100,000 inhabitants. He has kept a liberal economy, straightaway refused communism, and authorised the sale of a number of state-owned properties. Bolsonaro has abandoned the PT's foreign policy and has adopted different strategies; he has sought the Mercosur revision and strengthening ties with the US and other developed countries, whereas he has been cautious with the China's foreign policy. His far-right stance has fractured the social and political landscape in the country, and the absence of parliamentarian support has led Brazil to a state of ungovernability (Chagas-Bastos 2019, 93). In 2019 the economy grew marginally, even less than in 2017 and 2018, and the recovery since the 2015–2016 crisis has been disappointing. In this context, the popularity of Bolsonaro has decreased sharply.

Over the last 20 years Brazil's governments have transitioned across the right, the left, and the far right; in all these regimes, even in the left, the neoliberal orthodoxy and the inflation-targeting monetary policy has prevailed as the standard economic policy. The social police strategy has been diverse, but mainly focused on conditional cash transfer programmes and the universalisation of health and education public services. Adverse factors such as corruption and permanent debt and public deficits, besides dependence of the economy on international commodity prices and external markets such as China, have resulted in social, political, and economic difficulties that have inhibited sustained development. In this period, volatile economic growth and episodes of economic crisis persisted. The economic performance has been disappointing: between 1985 and 2018 the economy grew 2.58 per cent as a yearly average (Figure 4.5), while GDP per capita reached US$ 11,026 (constant 2010 US$), just a 40.23 per cent increase in real terms in 33 years (Figure 4.6). These figures are slightly better than those in Mexico but below Chile and Uruguay.

The poverty headcount ratio at US$ 5.50 per day (2011 PPP) as a percentage of population decreased substantially between 1981 and 2017, about 39.3 percentage points (see Figure 4.7), but Brazil is still a country with a high poverty rate (21.0 per cent). The poverty indicator is slightly below that of Mexico, but far above Chile and Uruguay. Moreover, the Gini indicator had a negligible drop over the same period, less than 5 points, while the figure is still high—53.3 (see Figure 4.8). This fact places Brazil as the most unequal of the four country case studies and one of the most unequal economies in the hemisphere.

To sum up, policies such as strategic trade openness, conducted on government industrial priorities and elites' lobbying, inflation targeting, and expansionary foreign policy in the PT's regime all performed within a

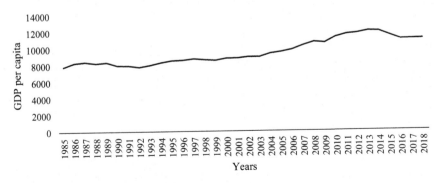

Figure 4.6 GDP per capita, constant 2010 US$ for Brazil
Source: World Bank (2020)

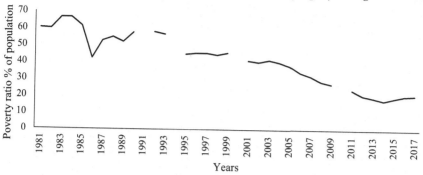

Figure 4.7 Poverty headcount ratio, US$ 5.50 per day (2011 PPP), percentage of population, Brazil
Source: World Bank (2020)

scenario of neoliberal orthodoxy, and did not form a basis for achieving sustained and equitable economic growth, as they created an imbalance of power between the financial markets, industrialists, corporations, and in general the capital on the one hand, and the labour sector on the other. As a result, the wages and the internal market remained depressed, and inequality remained high. In addition, the economy permanently struggled with debt and public deficits, and the budget was never sufficient to further reduce poverty and reverse the poor social conditions of the population. Despite the strategic liberalisation, the country has not achieved sound industrialisation. In the economic liberalisation era, strategies such as Lula's foreign policy favoured corporations concentrated on primary products, commodities, and civil construction, with affectations to natural resources and the environment, and hence, these policies have not encouraged sustained development. On the other hand, social programmes and gradual consolidation of liberal delegative democracy have contributed to marginally reduce poverty and inequality, and slightly improve the political rights indicator; between 1984 and 2019 it

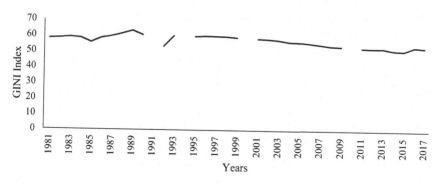

Figure 4.8 Gini index in Brazil (World Bank estimates)
Source: World Bank (2020)

moved from 3 to 2, and Brazil has moved to become a free country (Freedom House 2020).

Chile[2]

Human development in Chile has improved over the last two decades. The social and economic policies implemented in the 1980s and 1990s have placed Chile on a path of inclusive growth; nevertheless, the country faces economic difficulties. It relies heavily on export commodities and faces external volatility. Business confidence has declined, following a long period of rapid economic growth, and the economy since the end of 2012 has slowed down, mainly due to decreasing cooper prices and lower growth and demand from China.

The growth rate of exports (by volume) was not sufficient, even during the commodity boom, and there is an increasing trend of income elasticity of demand for imports, which is particularly high for China. The balance of payments position, hence, will continue to be the main growth constraint for Chile (Murakami and Hernández 2018). The increasing income elasticity of demand for imports and the balance of payments difficulties mainly occur because the country concentrates its exports on natural resources and primary production and has to import technology. The result is that people tend to import more and there is a persistent problem in the balance of payments.

The political context after the student revolt in 2011 and 2012 created the preconditions for re-initiated the progressive tax reform; political obstacles had limited it for the two decades following the return of democracy in 1990 (Fairfield 2015). In 2014 the government introduced tax reform aimed at raising its revenue as a share of GDP, financing an educational reform, improving the corporate tax system and the level of fairness of tax collection, and mitigating avoidance. The reform contributes to reduce regressivity, but deters investment owing to an increase in the corporate tax rate. Nowadays, the reform is fully in place, but the tax collection, as a percentage of GDP, is still significantly lower than the OECD average, and even low for Latin America.

The persistent lack of strength in Chile's productivity can be traced to weaknesses in the competitive scheme. The lack of a comprehensive regulatory reform has reduced the possibilities to achieve better economic outcomes and unleash resources to boost productivity. The low total factor productivity growth is partially linked to weaknesses in Chile's innovation system. This problematic is also associated with research and development spending (R&D), which remains low, particularly in the business sector.

To face low productivity and investment, the government has pursued different measures. An initial tax benefit for R&D expenditures was implemented in 2008 to promote private participation. A modification to this tax benefit in 2012 made in-house R&D activities eligible for the tax credit. After this modification, the flow of new applicants increased fivefold. Reforms over the past few years have made starting a business much easier. In May 2013, a new law to allow the opening of a business in one day took effect. The creation of the Start-Up Chile entrepreneurship programme in 2010, aims to make the country the leading innovation hub in Latin America, along with a number of complementary programmes that help to facilitate international technology transfer. The government has incorporated actions to expand the Start-Up Chile programme, and to ease SMEs access to credit through the Banco Estado.

Chile's performance in the Programme for International Student Assessment (PISA) improved in the early 2000s, but the pattern has slowed down recently and remains below the OECD average. The government has introduced major reforms to the education system. Access to primary and secondary education is above the average in Latin America, the access to tertiary education more than doubled between 2000 and 2015 and tertiary education is above the OECD average. Overall, the education system in Chile has achieved social benefits and is more efficient; indeed, it interrupts the cycle of inequality more than other Latin American country (Huerta-Wong 2012).

In terms of the healthcare system, Chile has achieved near universal health coverage, but it remains inequitable, because it is segmented, with services differing in quality, markedly worse on the public side, different costs and payments, and variations in benefits. The system relies mainly on payroll-based payments, which reduces incentives for formality. The private insurance market is also segmented and requires more regulation. The healthcare system has improved coverage, but its progressivity is still weak and has not become a determining factor in reducing inequality.

The high rate of economic growth in Chile, relative to Latin America and OECD countries, and the economic path of the country, have maintained a good labour market performance, particularly in terms of unemployment rates. On the other hand, there are important inequalities in the labour market. Women's labour market participation is among the lowest in OECD countries, youth face several difficulties in finding employment, and the market has a substantial proportion of workers in non-regular work arrangements. Informality, measured as the share of workers aged 15 to 64 years not contributing to the pension system, stood around 30 per cent over the last decade; the rate is low in Latin America but still high in the OECD. Inequality is exacerbated because pension contributions are particularly rare among low-income and self-employed workers.

Several reforms and programmes have been designed to improve the labour market conditions. In particular, attempts have been made to improve female employability, attract more women to the labour market, and address wage inequality. Improvements have also been made to provide training for the youth, to reduce employment costs for youth in the formal sector, and to incorporate low-skilled individuals and marginalised labour to the formal labour market. In addition, self-employed workers are required to contribute to their health insurance and pension funds. The labour reforms have helped to develop a collective bargaining process, benefiting both workers and firms, and to expand coverage of social protection.

Labour and pension reforms have made progress in alleviating elderly poverty, establishing an unemployment benefit through an individual savings accounts, and providing subsidies for working women. But transfers to the formal working class are less redistributive, because they exclude those in the informal sector. Nevertheless, the extent of redistribution in Chile is higher than in other countries in Latin America with a similar level of social spending.

Territorial disparities in Chile are high, when it comes to GDP, environmental quality, health, and housing. Not surprisingly the inter-regional Gini index is the largest in OECD countries, and centralisation is one of the most severe in the organisation. Bachelet's second administration launched a set of reforms to conduct a decentralisation and development agenda to address disparities by adopting public policies to attend local needs and opportunities. The reform agenda includes measures for modernising and strengthening the municipal system, as well as the government's goal of more inclusive and equitable growth.

Chile's strong economic growth with heavy reliance on natural resources has come at the cost of the environment. In 2013, revenues from environmental-related taxes represented 1.38 per cent of GDP. This figure is low compared to OECD countries. In order to increase public revenues for spending in environmental improvement areas and to create incentives for reducing CO_2 emissions, the government introduced a carbon tax that was set to start in 2018, as part of a comprehensive tax reform. It applies to the emissions of the power sector, and will gradually expand coverage to all sectors.

The political rights indicator in Chile is classified as free, with a value of 1. It is interesting to note that the indicator improved substantially from 1984 to 2020, as it moved from 6 to 1 (Freedom House 2020). The minimum wage has had marked improvements: it rose around 265 per cent between 1987 and 2019 in constant prices and is one of the largest in Latin America, but continues to be one of the smallest in the OECD (INE Chile 2020a). On the other hand, the tax–GDP ratio gained only 2.3 percentage points between 2000 and 2016 and passed from 18.8 per cent to 21.1 per cent—the improvement has been minimal and the tax income is still low (OECD 2020b); moreover, the percentage of the informal market remains high, 29.1 per cent in 2015, and with no change since 2009 (OECD 2018), while informal labour increased from 29.4 per cent in 2017, the year in which started the measure, to 30.4 per cent in 2019 (INE Chile 2020b).

In 2019 civil protests took place; they initiated due to a rise in Santiago's subway fare, but the protests and mass demonstration expanded rapidly throughout the country. The discontent was quickly fuelled by the severe inequality that persists in Chilean society and by the excessive use of force. Since the country's period of dictatorship, the country has transitioned peacefully between left and right regimes, but economic growth and the market liberalism have been unable to deliver the expected egalitarian

Figure 4.9 GDP growth, annual percentage for Chile
Source: World Bank (2020)

promises. As a result of the civil society movement, Congress signed an agreement to call a referendum in April 2020 aimed at asking voters their view on the enactment of a new Constitution.

Figures 4.9 and 4.10 show economic growth and GDP per capita in Chile between 1985 and 2018. The expansion of both indicators has been the highest of the four country case studies and one of the highest in Latin America. The former rose 4.95 per cent annually and the latter passed from US$ 4,697 to US$ 15,130 (constant 2010 US$) over the period, that is, an expansion of 222 per cent. Economic growth has been less volatile than in Mexico, Brazil, and Uruguay, but it is also unstable, with sharp falls in 1999 and 2009, slow down since 2013, and a rebound in 2018. It is worth noting that economic growth has maintained a decreasing trend over the period.

This volatility is the result of the liberal economic policy in Chile, which positions the country in a situation of dependence on international markets, and it is also the result of the high dependence the Chilean economy has on the commodity prices. Nevertheless, the fact that Chile has the lowest volatility,[3] out of the four case studies, suggests that regulations in capital flows— one of the economic policies distinguishing Chile in the hemisphere—have mitigated economic volatility.

Economic growth, despite volatility, and social policies have encouraged a sharp reduction in poverty, expressed as the poverty headcount ratio at a poverty line of US$ 5.50 per day (2011 PPP) as a percentage of the population. The ratio passed from 52.8 per cent to 6.4 per cent, between 1987 and 2017, as shown in Figure 4.11; in this sense, Chile has achieved the largest reduction in poverty, but Uruguay has the lowest level of poverty, out of the four economies.

In terms of income distribution, the Gini coefficient has dropped 10 points, from 56.2 to 46.6, between 1987 and 2017, as illustrated in Figure 4.12. It is the largest reduction in inequality in the four countries, but the country still remains an unequal one, and its Gini coefficient is larger than in Uruguay, but smaller than in Brazil and Mexico.

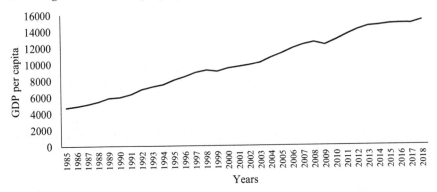

Figure 4.10 GDP per capita, constant 2010 US$ for Chile
Source: World Bank (2020)

To sum up, after 2000, Chile has continued to be a country with a democratic regime that prioritises human development and social benefits, establishing reforms in areas such as labour and pensions, and health and education. To achieve more equity, the government has launched a decentralisation agenda and tax reforms with a progressivity scheme. In addition, the country has consolidated the export-led growth model and placed special emphasis on fostering productivity and investment. During the last two decades, social movements have taken place, mainly boosted by the discontent that creates inequality; they have forced governments and Congress to adopt reforms, and more recently, to call for a constitutional referendum. The reforms continue to be negotiated in a top-down sense between the government, business elites and labour unions, but have also been motivated by the action of civil society. Overall, the country has kept the Post-Washington Consensus approach and a liberal economy, from the 1990s up to recent

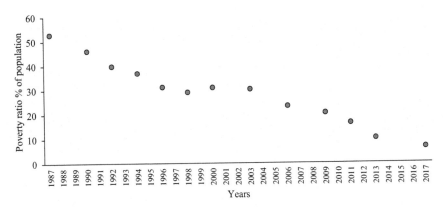

Figure 4.11 Poverty headcount ratio, US$ 5.50 per day (2011 PPP), percentage of
            population, Chile
Source: World Bank (2020)

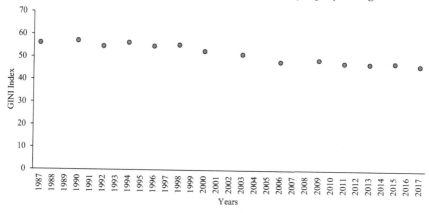

Figure 4.12 Gini index in Chile (World Bank estimates)
Source: World Bank (2020)

years, despite political alternation between left and right regimes. The Chilean model is associated with prominent economic and social performance, but also with persistent inequality, low productivity, economic volatility (although less than the other case studies), and a high informal sector.

Uruguay

From the election in 1970 and up to the election in 2004, the Broad Front (*Frente Amplio*), deemed a centre-left, pragmatic political party, gained popularity, while the two traditional parties, the Colorado Party (*Partido Colorado*) and the National Party (*Partido Nacional*), gradually lost support in the electoral results. The traditional bipartisan system changed bit by bit, and in the 2004 election was consolidated into a tripartite system. This result was also influenced by the economic crisis between 1999 and 2003, as it motivated the voters to explore an alternative option different than the traditional parties that were overcome by the crisis. The Broad Front defeated its adversaries in the 2009 and 2014 elections. Despite this transformation, the predominance of left-leaning political parties continues to mark Uruguay's political system.

The Broad Front has emphasised maintaining macroeconomic equilibria and low inflation, but also committed to trade and financial liberalisation, as the previous governments. It has also made progress in social, labour, and tax reforms, with distributive benefits towards the popular sectors and the middle class. The country continues to distinguish itself in the region due to its democratic and inclusive negotiation system. In this respect, along the first two Broad Front governments social expenditure has increased; the tripartite labour negotiations have led to wage improvements; the enactment of nearly 40 laws has expanded labour rights even to traditionally excluded sectors, such as rural and domestic workers; and the social protection scheme has tended to universalisation, especially in the health sector and transfers to families. In addition, the tax reform improved progressivity through income tax.

Fiscal policy in Uruguay plays an important role in ensuring low levels of inequality and poverty relative to Latin American standards. Direct (in-cash) transfers are progressive and contribute to reducing the average gap. In-kind transfers, especially public provision on education and healthcare, are usually provided for redistributive purposes; they are a higher proportion of public spending than in-cash transfers, and their contribution to narrowing gaps is more important than that of the direct transfers. Social programmes do not target specific ethnic groups; they are oriented to the most marginalised people. Nevertheless, they have reduced ethno-racial gaps and benefited afro-descendants and indigenous people to close the gap with whites (Bucheli et al. 2018).

The legal framework implemented by Uruguay in 1998, aimed at attracting foreign investment through general fiscal exemptions and the unrestricted transfers of profits and capital abroad, resulted in a considerable inflow of foreign capital that helped to mitigate the effects of the 2002 economic crises. The inflow of foreign investment has had a positive effect on productivity, skilled labour demand, and wages. However, Peluffo (2015) underlines the way it has led to greater wage inequality between skilled and unskilled labour; moreover, he points out that the growth of foreign investment occurred at a time of rising wage inequality, between the late 1990s and 2007, despite redistributive reforms implemented by centre-left governments. The legal framework for the operation of foreign investment in Uruguay has weaknesses, because it was designed to favour multinational corporations by creating tax-free and free-trade zones, and therefore does not regulate business conduct. In contrast, it reduces the bargaining power of civil society, legitimises the presence of corporations, and protect their interests. On these bases, Ehrnstrom-Fuentes and Kroger (2018) argue that the Uruguayan state's role and the role of multinational corporations exacerbates unequal power relations and does not set the conditions to create as many jobs as expected, and those created are usually of poor quality.

It should be added that after 2004, once the crisis of the beginning of the decade vanished, higher economic growth rates resumed and the social reforms of the Broad Front were conducted. Under these circumstances, income inequality began to drop, and poverty rates resumed their decreasing pace. Since then, both indicators have been dropping steadily (see Figures 4.15 and 4.16).

Uruguay's economic performance has been outstanding in the region over the last two decades, as the growth of both GDP and per-capita income have exceeded the Latin American averages, but it has been the most volatile out of the four country case studies, mainly owing to the economic crisis in Mexico in 1995 and in South America between 2000 and 2002 (see Figure 4.13). Moreover, since 2012, the slowdown of GDP growth in Brazil, with negative rates in 2015 and 2016, and the slower rates of growth in China, have impacted Uruguay's economy, which since then has recorded lower economic growth.

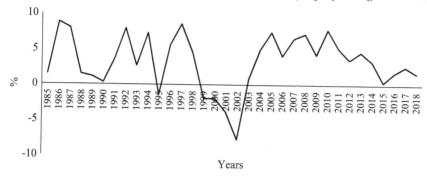

Figure 4.13 GDP growth, annual percentage for Uruguay
Source: World Bank (2020)

In 2019, as a result of lower commodity prices and the adverse context in the region, the economy of Uruguay only grew slightly. The country is highly dependent on external and regional economic factors, in particular on Mercosur and China's performance, while its development model, although socially successful, lacks further strategies to sustain economic growth.

In this context, internal consumption weakened, unemployment rose, and the inflationary pressure was higher; the inflation rate in 2015 reached 9.44 per cent, above the inflation target, ranging between 3 per cent and 7 per cent (Pérez and Piñeiro-Rodríguez 2016). Due to the adverse context, the tax revenue has tended to decline and the pressure on the public deficit and debt are more severe. Hence, the government has faced the dilemma of maintaining sound public finances with low public expenditure or responding to the social demands of greater distribution of income and welfare of the population, but jeopardising macroeconomic balance. The latter demands come mainly from the unions, which have real bargaining power in Uruguay and are the social base of the government.

Despite these economic difficulties in Uruguay in recent years, and the effect of liberal investment policies on wage inequality, the Broad Front, like previous governments from the two traditional parties, has managed to keep macroeconomic equilibria, while its public policy has been oriented towards the left wing and towards progressive strategies. In addition, the unions continue to cooperate with the state, capital, and parties in coalitions supporting import substitution, but with a substantial degree of autonomy. This social and political coalition has also kept some form of resistance to liberalism as the labour confederation has induced resistance to full privatisation of the pension system.[4] This fact shows that welfare entitlements and provisions are widely disseminated in society, and political parties and social actors have resisted fully implementing neoliberal reforms, while they have adopted welfare policies that upheld established social rights (Grassi 2014). Overall, the last three governments have kept the traditional propensity in Uruguay to

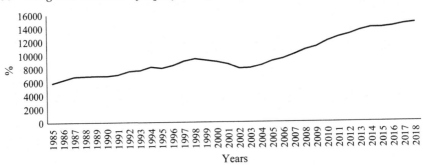

Figure 4.14 GDP per capita, constant 2010 US$ for Uruguay
Source: World Bank (2020)

build the Latin American version of the welfare state and to rule with participatory democracy.

In terms of economic and social performance, Uruguay has improved in many aspects in recent years. Informal employment, although still high, declined by 17 percentage points in a decade, between 2004 and 2014, from 40.7 to 23.5 as a percentage of total employment (CEPAL 2016). Since then, the figures have remained steady, according to statistics from the World Bank (2020). The minimum wage increased 314 per cent between 2004 and 2019 (INE 2019), and currently has the largest minimum wage in Latino America. Tax revenue as a percentage of GDP, although it is still low, has expanded from 14.7 to 20.1 per cent between 2000 and 2018 (World Bank 2020). The political rights indicator, a proxy of the status of democracy in a country, has a scale of 1 to 7 (1 being the best position), and with a value of 1, Uruguay is classified as free. It should be added that the indicator improved substantially from 1984 to 2020, as it moved from 5 to 1 (Freedom House 2020).

The Uruguayan model and the economic and social performance of the country are associated with faster GDP (though volatile) and GDP per capita

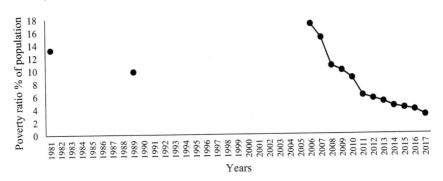

Figure 4.15 Poverty headcount ratio, US$ 5.50 a day (2011 PPP), percentage of population, Uruguay
Source: World Bank (2020)

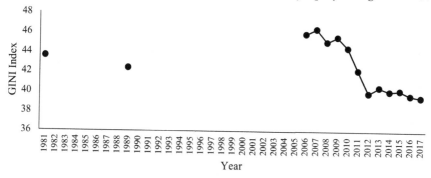

Figure 4.16 Gini index in Uruguay (World Bank estimates)
Source: World Bank (2020)

growth than the Latin American average, and decreasing poverty and inequality.

In 2019, the centre-right party defeated the Broad Front, after 15 years in power. This transition is mainly explained by the null economic growth in 2019 and the deterioration of the economy over the last eight years—in other words the Broad Front's governments were worn down in a natural process. In addition, the instability of leftist governments in the region, notably in Brazil, Venezuela, and Bolivia, discredited the leftist regimes.

Figure 4.13 and Figure 4.14 show GDP growth and GDP per capita between 1985 and 2017, respectively. In the former, it can be seen that economic growth has been volatile, with sharp drops in 1988–1990, 1995, 1999–2003, and 2015; on average, annual GDP growth in the period was 3.24 per cent; it can be seen that GDP per capita increased from US$ 5,873 to US$ 14,617 in the period, that is, 149 per cent in real terms over 32 years, with a fall between 1999 and 2002, because of the crisis in Brazil and Argentina. The growth of both indicators in Uruguay has been higher than in Mexico and Brazil and slower than in Chile. Uruguay, although less immersed in globalisation than Mexico, has also been affected by international volatility; in fact, its economic growth is the most volatile out of the four countries.[5]

The poverty headcount ratio, at US$ 5.50 a day (2011 PPP) as a percentage of population, is presented in Figure 4.15, for the period 1981–2017. As commented before, we use the same indicator for the four country case studies because it is comparable among them, and not the poverty ratio at national poverty line, because it changes from country to country. The indicator has declined from 13.2 to 2.9 per cent, more than 10 percentage points during the period, and it is the lowest out of the four countries. The crisis of 1999–2002 severely affected the poverty levels, but after this period the indicator has declined sharply, showing that poverty is close to being eradicated in Uruguay.

In 36 years, between 1981 and 2017, the Gini coefficient fell by 9 per cent, from 43.6 to 39.5, as presented in Figure 4.16. It has been a significant improvement in terms of income distribution in Uruguay, as the indicator has reached the lowest figure out of the four countries. The drop of the Gini coefficient was particularly rapid after the 1999–2002 crisis and up to 2012.

Overall, Uruguay has liberalised trade and the inflow of foreign investment, but has kept scenarios of resistance to fully liberalise some aspects of the economy, especially in what concerns labour issues and the national pension scheme. Besides, the country has adopted a welfare state model, with participatory democracy and the involvement of civil society and national actors in the decision-making process. The liberal policy had an adverse effect on inequality at the beginning of the century, mainly for the inflow of foreign investment, and has contributed to generating volatility in economic growth, owing to the instability in regional and international markets. Nevertheless, the country, due to the effect of public policies, has managed to reduce poverty and inequality to the lowest levels in Latino America and to keep economic growth above the average in the subcontinent. On the other hand, the Uruguayan governments require the development of innovative economic policies to sustain growth, which has decelerated since 2012 and faced a more complicated scenario in 2019. Eventually, this fact led to the transition from the left to the centre-right in the presidential election in 2019.

In this chapter we have analysed the political economy and the economic and social performance of the four countries over a long period (two decades in this chapter) or in a longer-run context; in the next chapter, we provide a summary of the main conclusions, as well as policy implications, and the challenges the governments in the region face to succeed within conditions of economic openness.

Notes

1 In 2000 the National Action Party (PAN) came into power, after 71 years of political hegemony of the Institutional Revolutionary Party (PRI). After 12 years of PAN governments, in 2012 the PRI returned to the presidency, and six years later, in 2018, the leftist MORENA party came to power.
2 This section of the book mainly relies on OECD (2015).
3 The volatility measure is obtained by computing the variance of the annual GDP rate of growth, in real terms, between 1985 and 2018, using World Bank (2020) statistics.
4 The traditional public pension system, managed by the state, gave way to a mixed system that integrated private companies and a complementary capitalisation arrangement for the upper income sectors; these changes deeply transformed the old system, but it has remained statist and coherent with social goals abandoned by other regional governments.
5 The volatility measure is obtained by computing the variance of the annual GDP rate of growth, in real terms, between 1985 and 2018, using World Bank (2020) statistics.

5 Final remarks

Between the mid-1980s and the late 1990s, the period of adjustment and Washington Consensus (WC) reforms in Latin America, the region in general registered modest and unstable rates of economic growth, while poverty was still largely endemic and income redistribution was not achieved. Nevertheless, economic liberalisation is unlikely to be abandoned. The increasing participation of Latin American countries in bilateral and regional trade agreements reduces possibilities of restraining economic liberalisation. Furthermore, the Uruguayan case revealed that resistance to economic liberalisation and resistance to private capital investment can result in fiscal problems and financial difficulties; the Brazilian case illustrated that *strategic* trade openness, led by elites' lobbying and government industrial priorities does not promote sustained economic growth and generates issues around corruption. On the other hand, openness was not the real problem since countries worst affected by market-oriented policies are those in which inappropriate economic policies, macroeconomic disequilibria and social and political obstacle were more accentuated.

The shorth-run experience of economic liberalisation in the country case studies shows that the fundamental challenge of the Latin American state, within an economic liberalisation context, is how to participate in the global economy without affecting domestic economic stability. The Mexican case illustrates the destabilising effects on exports and growth caused by a rapid capital account liberalisation and a huge infusion of short-term investment; in contrast, the Chilean case shows that regulation of short-term investment is not only feasible, but also desirable for mitigating financial turbulence and achieving greater macroeconomic stability. Furthermore, tightening banking supervision and improving economic management have also been worthy policies in the region. Hence, economic liberalisation needs to be accompanied by domestic macroeconomic efficiency and prudential regulation and supervision in areas such as banking and short-run investment in order to reduce economic volatility. Moreover, the Latin American state needs to undertake pragmatic and subtle economic liberalisation, that is, placing special emphasis on strengthening domestic markets, reducing economic volatility, and avoiding powerlessness of vulnerable sectors.

The Brazilian and Chilean early experience in liberalisation reveals two models in which the mechanism of prices and market forces were not unique strategies to adjust exports to comparative advantages. In this context, Chile effectively undertook economic intervention of the state through cooperative arrangements among business, bureaucrats, and trade unions; and continuity of specific projects targeted during the import substitution industrialisation (ISI) epoch as a developmental strategy for boosting comparative advantages. On the other hand, the Chilean experience notes that the predefined Latin American comparative advantages mainly oriented to reliance on natural resources does not form the basis for sustained exports and economic growth. As for Brazil, strategic trade openness and state intervention inherited from the ISI model were conducted through the involvement of government and business elites, but lacked more participatory scenarios, including the active role of civil society and labour. This developmental strategy failed to achieve sustained economic growth and to some extent, resulted in social imbalance and discontent.

Therefore, the state in the region not only needs to conduct developmental actions for fostering predefined comparative advantages, but also needs to undertake participatory consensus among different actors, further developmental forms of organisation, and specific government intervention in order to achieve inclusion, industrialisation, the development of new competitive advantages, less reliance on natural resources, and more effective use of them.[1]

By the late 1990s, heavy reliance on public investment and resistance to privatisation were determining causes of the financial problems in Uruguay, whereas lack of transparency and emphasis on capital concentration in the Mexican privatisation process did not contribute to improve economic conditions. In this respect, the Chilean experience provides an important alternative, since privatisation oriented toward '*capitalismo popular*' represented a real option of the state for further privatisation in the region.

Macroeconomic equilibrium, popular privatisation, development forms of organisation, large-scale industrialisation, prudential regulation and supervision in vulnerable economic activities, and subtle and pragmatic economic liberalisation are essential strategies that the state cannot ignore in order to achieve sustained export growth, sustained economic expansion, and poverty alleviation. Nevertheless, these strategies need to be complemented with a set of sociopolitical norms that include civil society participation, social and human capital formation, effective democratic regulation, transparency, and accountability in order to reduce income inequality.

To some extent, in the early stage of economic liberalisation and up to the late 1990s, Chile adopted this set of sociopolitical norms, but the Chilean case did not account for improvement in income distribution. In this sense, the understanding of democratisation, participation, and incorporation are crucial. In the Chilean polyarchy, despite consensus among the main actors, there still exists a disproportional distribution of power in society, whereas the incorporation of civil society and NGOs was controlled from above; hence income redistribution was inhibited. On the other hand, Uruguay also adopted a broad notion of sociopolitical norms; in addition, its participatory democracy aggregated major social demands since civil society has real bargaining power, and incorporation of sociopolitical actors was exerted in a bottom-up sense. As a result, this model attained better levels of income distribution. Nevertheless, in the Uruguayan democracy, the clientelist system functioned as a cohesive mechanism of popular aggregation that generated high resistance to liberalisation and jeopardised long-term stability. In summary, the state not only needs to promote incorporation from below, but also needs to replace clientelist forms of organisation by consensus, negotiation, and greater consciousness in civil society, political parties, and the government. In this way, the state can promote subtle and pragmatic economic liberalisation compatible with income distribution.

The WC prescription is an incomplete development model. It showed serious limitations in the Mexican economy up to the late 1990s and even after. The Latin American state can humanise and complement market dynamics and the original neoliberal prescription by adopting the Post-Washington Consensus (PWC) approach. However, if the state wants to tackle the high degree of inequality that characterises the region, it has to concede more ground to themes such as the developmental state, the Keynesian approach, the balance of payments constrained growth model, and the growth of domestic markets; as well as an effective participatory democracy and incorporation from below.

These socioeconomic ideas were not only policy options for Latin America during the late1990s; they were trends in the region and were adopted by some countries at different levels. In the four country case studies, Uruguay attached more to the sociopolitical norms, followed by Chile, and then Brazil, while Mexico barely adopted them. In this context, Higgott and Phillips hold that a hegemonic neoliberal discourse moved toward a reconstituted Keynesianism and this represented a late-1990s buzzword in the Latin American press. Moreover, they also note that Keynesian ideas became useful intellectual pegs on which Latin American governments did hang certain policies (Higgott and Phillips 2000, 370, 373). This trend constituted a complement to neoliberal economic principles. In addition, the persistent social struggle and the resistance that characterise the region attempt to equalise balance of power among social actors and to encourage participation and incorporation from below. This trend in the transition toward democratisation was not consistent with the incorporation in a top-down sense that the PWC rhetoric advocates. Although Latin American states by the late 1990s adopted a number of features consistent with the neoliberal orthodoxy and the PWC approach, the scope of the political economy of the epoch in the region was not in keeping with the policy convergence that multilateral financial institutions and Anglo-Saxon states promote.

The persistent economic crises that swept the region during the 1980s and 1990s, and unstable economic growth, showed some of the risks of globalisation. If economic liberalisation is unlikely to be abandoned, the Latin American states have to attempt to correct the adverse mechanism of trade and investment that prevails on a global scale, otherwise domestic efforts can be overshadowed by global forces. In negotiation rounds of the World Trade Organization (WTO), Latin American states have not constituted a block in order to improve their bargaining power. This fact is a common practice in different global forums. Consequently, states in the region need to constitute a homogeneous group so as to cope with the global problems of under-representation and economic polarisation, and to attain fair mechanisms of trade and investment.

Over the longer run and up to recent years, the four countries have transitioned across different regimes, they all have experienced left and the right governments, but have tended to keep economic liberalisation policies. Despite the rhetoric of some regimes, which have claimed to be leftist and reject neoliberalism, the PT in Brazil and the last Mexican government for instance, the case studies presented in this book show that the neoliberal economic orthodoxy has tended to consolidate in the four countries, under different conditions of social policy, level of inclusion, and openness strategy.

The political economy of market liberalism in Latin America has been diverse across countries and over time; nevertheless, the four country case studies encompass most of the economic models in the region; except those which have adopted statist or central planning models.

Mexico, even in the current leftist government, is still attached to the WC model, and strong presidentialism. The party system prevails, and delegative democracy is maintained, while the social programmes remain clientelist and weak, social aggregation is conducted from above, and the bargaining power of capital is dominant. The investment and trade approach is one of the most liberal in the region, and the country continues to rely on manufacturing and maquila, but has been unable to consolidate its own industry. The country has adopted fiscal discipline and sound macroeconomic policies, but maintain the large-scale informal market, low tax revenue, and economic volatility. The result is slow economic growth, marginal reduction of poverty and inequality with persistent high levels, and weak political rights.

Brazil conducted WC economic policies with some variations; trade openness was undertaken on the basis of government industrial priorities, elites' lobbying, and strategic industrialisation; that is, in the economic liberalisation era, trade policies showed reluctance to fully abandon the ISI approach. Either in the inclusive liberalism or in the neo-developmentalism regimes, governments adopted some sociopolitical norms advocated by the PWC model in the sense that they implemented conditional cash transfer programmes and attempted to universalise health and education public services. Delegative democracy has not evolved to more participatory forms, while political rights tend to consolidate. The post-neoliberal regionalism strategy resulted in corruption scandals and more capital concentration. The Brazilian case rendered low economic growth and a reduction in poverty, but still maintains high levels in the latter; although in both variables the country achieved slightly better results than Mexico. Structural problems such as high inequality, large proportion of informal economy, and significant reliance on natural resources persist.

Chile is more associated with a PWC model, as it is a liberal country with a consolidation of social policies and a liberal democracy; social aggregation is also from above, and economic and political elites continue to take the most important decisions in the country, though there is some evidence of bargaining power of labour and civil society. The country has targeted strategic projects aimed at boosting comparative advantages, and innovation and industrial diversification have achieved substantial improvements, but the country still relies heavily on primary production. Chile has kept regulatory controls in the short-term capital flows, and remains the least volatile economy in comparison to the other case studies. The country faces low tax revenue and a large proportion of informal markets in the economy. This model has resulted in rapid economic growth, with episodes of instability and deceleration in recent years, reduction of poverty, consolidated political rights, and persistent inequality.

Uruguay continues to be a participatory democracy with consolidated social policies and programmes. Although the country has liberalised more sectors of the economy, it is still reluctant to intensify the privatisation of state-owned firms, and to fully liberalise the economy and the pension scheme. As some other countries in the region, Uruguay maintains strong dependence on primary production. The tax revenue is low and the informal sector is large, as is the case in other Latin American countries. The model is associated with moderate and volatile economic growth, consolidated political rights, significant reductions in poverty, and less inequality than most of the countries in the region.

After more than three decades or so of economic liberalisation in Latin America, Mexico and Brazil have showed slow rates of economic growth, while Chile and Uruguay presented more economic expansion, but still insufficient for an emerging economy; in any case, economic volatility persists. This result is associated with a large proportion of informal labour market, low tax revenue, lack of external market diversification, and heavy reliance on primary production, maquila, and manufacturing intensive in labour. Mexico, Brazil, and Chile face high levels of inequality, while Uruguay seems to overcome this problem gradually.

Table 5.1 presents a summary of indictors from the four case studies—growth, economic volatility, poverty, and inequality—over the last three decades or so and with the latest available figures.

The approaches of economic liberalisation in the region range from models strongly attached to the Washington Consensus with little social emphasis, to models involving effective regulatory policies, strategic project targeting, and some restrictions on economic liberalisation, besides inclusive social policy and participatory democracy, even overcoming the prescription advocated by

Table 5.1 Summary of indicators on economic growth, volatility, poverty, and inequality

Indicators	Mexico	Brazil	Chile	Uruguay
GDP growth, annual average (%), 1985–2018	2.45	2.58	4.95	3.24
Volatility of GDP annual growth, 1995–2018	8.16	8.48	7.20	14.37
GDP per capita, 2018 (constant 2010 US$)	10,403	11,026	15,130	14,617
GDP per capita growth (constan 2010 US$), in the period 1985–2018, (%)	32.16	40.23	222.09	148.88
* GINI index (last year)	48.3	53.3	46.6	39.5
* Poverty headcount ratio at $5.50 a day (2011 PPP) (% of population) (last year)	25.7	21.0	6.4	2.9

Source: Own computation with information from World Bank (2020) Notes: *Brazil, Chile, and Uruguay 2017, Mexico 2016
Country with the best performance in the specific indicator
Country with the worst performance in the specific indicator

the PWC. Those countries, leaning towards the first model have been less successful, in social and economic terms, and are lagging behind; in contrast, those countries leaning towards the second model have achieved better social conditions and economic performance, but still present limitations and are far from the GDP per capita of developed countries. In any case, there is room for improvement. Figure 5.1 illustrates the performance of the countries and the models they have adopted.

In order to achieve sustained and high rates of economic growth, according to the four case studies explored in this book, the countries in the region have to conduct an integral economic policy consisting of strategic points, such as the promotion of a national competitive industry capable of surviving in global markets and suitable of substituting imports. The industrialisation has to be fostered by the state leadership, targeting strategic sectors, in which both comparative and competitive advantages can be boosted, through consensus and strong alliance incorporating the private and the labour sectors, academic institutions, and civil society; without jeopardising public finance and ensuring efficiency, productivity, and transparency. The industrialisation of the economy boosts the formalisation of markets and therefore the expansion of tax revenue (Angeles-Castro and Ramírez-Camarillo 2014, 40–41).

Latin American nations have persistently struggled with current account deficits; in the economic liberalisation era, the countries in the sample have had to cope with the problem through restrictive fiscal policy and inflation-targeting monetary regimes. This fact has restricted growth and maintained inequality. In the logic of Thirlwall's law, emphasis on industrialisation improves the balance of payments conditions and allows more economic growth. Moreover, within the Keynesian approach, industrialisation can achieve income redistribution.

The privatisation of non-strategic state-owned firms in the logic of '*capitalismo popular*', in order to reduce capital concentration, is also desirable. It has to be undertaken through a transparent processes, avoiding corruption and corporativism, and ensuring sustainability and financial viability of the firms. The resources obtained in this process should be allocated to infrastructure, education, and health, and be devoted to reducing poverty and inequality, and not to current expenditure or short-term investments.

So as to reinforce tax collection and the formality of the economy, the Latin American state is required to conduct fiscal policy reforms oriented to increase the tax base and the incorporation of informal labour to the social security system, by diversifying the contributions to the system and reducing the burden on the beneficiaries and the entrepreneurs. Progressive tax policies can help to mitigate inequality.

In order to reduce volatility and achieve sustained economic growth, Latin American countries are required to regulate the flow of volatile investments, following the experience of Chile, and to reduce significant dependence on primary production and commodities. The region also needs to diversify markets to avoid dependence on specific countries such as China and the United States.

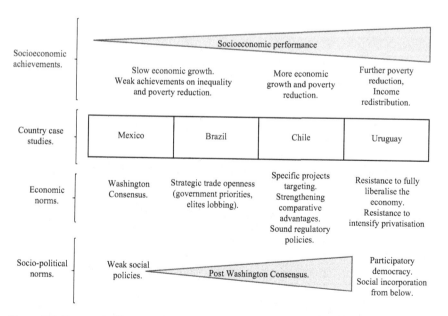

Figure 5.1 Economic liberalisation style and socioeconomic performance

The inclusion of participatory democracy and society in the decision-making process in a bottom-up sense, as in the Uruguayan experience, the adoption of legal mechanisms such as plebiscite and referendum, and the reduction of disproportionate power of presidentialism and the party systems can boost the balance of power, the redistribution of income, and access to social benefits, and can provide more opportunities for those in need.

The achievement of less economic volatility and better levels of income distribution in Latin America require policy convergence in order to constitute a block that achieves autonomy and greater bargaining power on a global scale. Therefore, the challenge of the state, in a market liberalism context, is not confined to a domestic scope, since it also involves regional and global actions. To the extent that Latin America as a region converges in a sound single model, it will be more feasible to cope with global and inter-regional problems, and to achieve a fair position on a global scale.

Note

1 Lessons from the ISI model suggest that state intervention in the economy and active industrial policy can yield negative results. However, under improved socio-political conditions and reinvigorated institutions, industrial policy and state intervention can provide better results. In addition, large-scale industrialisation in the ISI model was not capable of absorbing the full labour force, but complementing industrialisation with predefined comparative advantages can offer more possibilities for employment, sustained economic growth, and income redistribution.

References

Agosin, Manuel R. and French-Davis, Ricardo (1995) 'Trade Liberalization and Growth: Recent Experiences in Latin America', *Journal of Interamerican Studies and World Affairs*, 37:3, pp. 9–57.

Alarcón, Diana and McKinley, Terry (1998) 'Increasing Wage Inequality and Trade Liberalization in Mexico', in Albert Barry, ed., *Poverty, Economic Reform, and Income Distribution in Latin America*. Boulder, CO: Lynne Rienner Publishers, pp. 137–153.

Angeles-Castro, Gerardo (2007) 'Factors Driving Changes in Income Distribution in Post-Reform Mexico', University of Kent, Department of Economics, Discussion Paper 07/06.

Angeles-Castro, Gerardo and Ramírez-Camarillo, Diana Berenice (2014) 'Determinants of Tax Revenue in OECD Countries over the Period 2001–2011', *Contaduría y Administración*, 59:3, pp. 35–59.

Arestis, Philip and Saad-Filho, Alfredo (2007) 'Introduction', in Philip Arestis and Alfredo Saad-Filho, eds, *Political Economy of Brazil*. Hampshire: Palgrave Macmillan, pp. 1–6.

Arruda de Almeida, Monica (2004) *What Prevents Economic Liberalisation? The Political Economy of Trade Protectionism*, Doctor of Philosophy in Political Science Thesis. Los Angeles, CA: University of California.

Avritzer, Leonardo (2017) 'The Impeachment of Dilma Rousseff: Introduction', *Critical Policy Studies*, 11:3, pp. 349–351.

Bailey, David, Harte, George, and Sugden, Roger (1998) 'Debate: Transnational Corporations. The Case for a Monitoring Policy Across Europe', *New Political Economy*, 3:2, pp. 279–300.

Banco de México (2001) *Información Financiera*. Mexico City. http://www.banxico.org.mx/eInfoFinanciera.

Barbosa dos Santos, Fabio Luis (2019) 'Neo-Development of Underdevelopment: Brazil and the Political Economy of South American Integration under the Worker´s Party', *Globalizations*, 16:2, pp. 216–231.

Barrett, Patrick S. (2001) 'Labour Policy, Labour-Business Relations and the Transition to Democracy in Chile', *Journal of Latin American Studies*, 33, pp. 561–597.

Barton, Jonathan R. (1999) 'Chile', in J. Buxton and N. Phillips, eds, *Case Studies in Latin American Political Economy*. Manchester: Manchester University Press, pp. 62–81.

Berry, Albert (1998a) 'Confronting the Income Distribution Threat in Latin America', in Albert Barry, ed., *Poverty, Economic Reform, and Income Distribution in Latin America*. Boulder, CO: Lynne Rienner Publishers, pp. 9–41.

Berry, Albert (1998b) 'Introduction', in Albert Barry, ed., *Poverty, Economic Reform, and Income Distribution in Latin America*. Boulder, CO: Lynne Rienner Publishers, pp. 1–5.

Blecker, Robert A. (2015) 'The Mexican and the US Economies after Twenty Years of NAFTA', *International Journal of Political Economy*, 43:2, pp. 5–26.

Borensztein, E., De Gregorio, J., and Lee, J-W. (1998) 'How Does Foreign Direct Investment Affect Economic Growth?' *Journal of International Economics*, 45, pp. 115–135.

Brewer, Anthonu (1990) *Marxist Theories of Imperialism: a Critical Survey*, 2nd edn. London: Routledge.

Bucheli, Marisa, Rossi, Maximo, and Amábile, Florencia (2018) 'Inequality and Fiscal Policies in Uruguay by Race', *The Journal of Economic Inequality*, published online, pp. 1–23.

Carrera-Troyano, Miguel and Domínguez-Martín, Rafael (2017) 'Poverty Reduction in Brazil and Mexico. Growth, Inequality and Public Policies', *Revista de Economía Mundial*, 45, pp. 23–42.

Central Bank of Chile (2002) *Base de Datos Economicos de la Balanza Comercial*. Santiago de Chile. www.bcentral.cl/indicadores/excel/balanza_comercial.xls.

CEPAL (2016) *El Proceso de Formalización en el Mercado Laboral Uruguayo*. Montevideo, Uruguay.

Chagas-Bastos, Fabrício H. (2019) 'Political Realignmnet in Brazil: Jair Bolsonaro and the Right Turn', *Revista de Estudios Sociales*, 69, pp. 92–100.

Cook, Maria Lorena (1997) 'Regional Integration and Transnational Politics: Popular Sector Strategies in the NAFTA era', in Douglas A. Chalmers, ed., *The New Politics of Inequality in Latin America: Rethinking Participation and Representation*. Oxford: Oxford University Press, pp. 516–540.

CONASAMI (2020) *Salario Mínimo Histórico 1877–2019, Mexico*. https://datos.gob.mx/busca/dataset/salario-minimo-historico-1877-2019.

Cox, Robert W. (1992) 'Multilateralism and World Order', *Review of International Studies*, 18:2, pp. 161–180.

ECLAC (1997) *The Equity GAP: Latin America, the Caribbean and the Social Summit*. Santiago, Chile: United Nations Publication.

ECLAC (2002) *Social Panorama of Latin America*. Santiago, Chile: United Nations Publication.

ECLAC (2004) *Social Panorama of Latin America*. Santiago, Chile: United Nations Publication.

Ehrnstrom-Fuentes, María and Kroger, Markus (2018) 'The Role of the State in Forestry Politics and Development in Uruguay', *Journal of Rural Studies*, 57, pp. 197–208.

El Mundo al Revés (2002) 'Crónica de una Muerte Anunciada', *Indymedia Uruguay*, 1 August, p. 1. http://uruguay.indymedia.org/news/2002/08/4488.php.

Fairfield, Tasha (2015) 'La Economía Política de la Reforma Tributaria Progresiva en Chile', *Revista de Economía Institucional*, 17:32, pp. 129–156.

Fernández, Raul (1996) 'The New Financial Regime in Latin America', in Victor Bulmer-Thomas, ed., *The New Economic Model in Latin America and Its Impact on Income Distribution and Poverty*. London: Macmillan Press, pp. 103–125.

Ferreira, Alfonso and Tullio Giuseppe (2002) 'The Brazilian Exchange Rate Crisis of January 1999', *Journal of Latin American Studies*, 34, pp. 143–164.

Filgueira, F. and J. Papadópulos (1997) 'Putting conservatism to good use? Long crisis and vetoed alternatives in Uruguay', in Douglas A. Chalmers, Carlos M.

Vilas, Katherine Hite, Scott B. Martin, Kerianne Piester, and Monique Segarra, eds, *The New Politics of Inequality in Latin America*. Oxford: Oxford University Press.

FitzGerald, E. V. K. (1996) 'The New Trade Regime: Macroeconomic Behaviour and Income Distribution in Latin Amercia', in Victor Bulmer-Thomas, ed., *The New Economic Model in Latin America and Its Impact on Income Distribution and Poverty*. London: Macmillan Press, pp. 29–52.

Freedom House (2020) *Data and Resources*. Washington, DC. https://freedomhouse. org/report/countries-world-freedom-2019.

Gilpin, Robert (1987) *The Political Economy of International Relations*. Princeton, NJ; Oxford: Princeton University Press.

Grassi, Davide (2014) 'Democracy and Social Welfare in Uruguay and Paraguay', *Latin American Politics and Society*, 56:1, pp. 120–143.

Griffith-Jones, Stephany (1996) 'International Capital Flows to Latin America', in Victor Bulmer-Thomas, ed., *The New Economic Model in Latin America and Its Impact on Income Distribution and Poverty*. London: Macmillan Press, pp. 127–143.

Grugel, Jean (1998) 'State and Business in Neoliberal Democracies in Latin America', *Global Society*, 12:2, pp. 221–235.

Gwynne, R. (1999) 'Globalization, Neoliberalism and Economic Change in South America and Mexico' in R. Gwynne and C. Key, eds., *Latin America Transformed: Globalization and Modernity*. London: Arnold, pp. 68–97.

Hay, Colin (2000) 'Contemporary Capitalism, Globalization, Regionalization and the Persistence of National Variation', *Review of International Studies*, 26, pp. 509–531.

Heath, Jonathan E. (1998) 'The Impact of Mexico's Trade Liberalization', in Carol Wise, ed., *The Post-Nafta Political Economy: Mexico and the Western Hemisphere*. University Park, PA: Pennsylvania State University Press, pp. 171–200.

Helleiner, Eric (2002) 'Economic Nationalism as a Challenge to Economic Liberalism? Lessons from the 19th Century', *International Studies Quarterly*, 46, pp. 307–329.

Helwege, Ann (1995) 'Poverty in Latin America: Back to the Abyss', *Journal of Interamerican Studies and World Affairs*, 37:3, pp. 99–123.

Hernández-Rodríguez, Job (2015) 'México: Cambio Económico sin Democracia', *Estudios Latinoamericanos*, 34, pp. 95–116.

Higgott, Richard (2000) 'Contested Globalization: the Changing Context and Normative Challenges', *Review of International Studies*, 26, 131–153.

Higgott, Richard and Phillips, Nicola (2000) 'Challenging Triumphalism and Convergence: the Limits of Global Liberalization in Asia and Latin America', *Review of International Studies*, 26, pp. 359–379.

Hojman, David (1994) 'The Political Economy of Recent Conversions to Market Economics in Latin America', *Journal of Latin American Studies*, 26:1, pp. 191–219.

Huerta-Wong, Juan Enrique (2012) 'El Rol de la Educación en la Movilidad Social de México y Chile', *Revista Mexicana de Investigación Educativa*, 17:52, pp. 65–88.

INE (2019) *Precios y Salarios*. Uruguay. http://www.ine.gub.uy/web/guest/salario-m inimo-nacional.

INE Chile (2020a) *Estadísticas Laborales*. Santiago, Chile. http://www.ine.cl/estadistica s/laborales/ene.

INE Chile (2020b) *Informalidad y Condiciones Laborales*, Santiago, Chile. https://www. ine.cl/estadisticas/sociales/mercado-laboral/informalidad-y-condiciones-laborales.

Instituto Nacional de Estadística Geográfica e Informática (2002) http://www.inegi. gob.mx.

Instituto Nacional de Estadística Geográfica e Informática (2020) *Medición de la Economía Informal Base 2013, Participación de la Economía Informal en el PIB, México City.* https://www.inegi.org.mx/temas/pibmed/.

International Labour Organization (1998) *World Employment Report 1998–99, Employability in the Global Economy: How Training Matters.* Geneva: International Labour Office.

International Labour Organization (2000) *World Labour Report 2000, Income security and Social Protection in a Changing World.* Geneva: International Labour Office.

Jardón, Eduardo and Román, Romina (2001) 'Critican Superpeso; Rechaza SHCP que Haya Sobreevaluacion', *El Universal,* 5 December, p. 5.

Kaztman, R., Filgueira, F., and Furtado, M. (2000) 'New Challenges for Equity in Uruguay', *CEPAL Review,* 72, pp. 79–98.

Kirby, Peadar (2002) 'The World Bank or Polany: Markets, Poverty and Social Well-being in Latin America', *New Political Economy* 7:2, pp. 199–219.

Kume, Honório, Guida, Piani, and Bráz de Souza, Carlos F. (2001) 'A Política de Importação no Period 1987–1998: Descrição e Avaliação', manuscript. Rio de Janeiro: IPEA.

Leubolt, Bernhard (2014) 'Social Policies and Redistribution in Brazil', Global Labour University, Working Paper 14/26.

Lipset, Seymour Martin (1960) *Political Man.* London: Heinemann.

López, Teresa S., Mantey, Guadalupe, and Quintana, Luis (2012) 'Exchange Rate Pass-through Inflation and Wage Differentials in Late-Industrializing Economies: the Mexican Case', *Brazilian Journal of Political Economy,* 32:4, pp. 634–655.

Mishkin, Frederic S. (1996) *'Understanding Financial Crises: A Developing Country Perspective',* Annual World Bank Conference on Development Economics, The World Bank, pp. 29–77.

Morley, Samuel A., (1995) *Poverty and Inequality in Latin America: The Impact of Adjustment and Recovery in the 1980s.* Baltimore, MD: Johns Hopkins University Press.

Muñoz-Martínez, Hepzibah (2008) *The State and the Internationalisation of Capital: The Mexican Territoriality of Global Finance, 1982–2006,* Doctor of Philosophy Thesis. Toronto, Canada: York University.

Murakami, Yoshimichi and Hernández, René A. (2018) 'The Impacts of China on Economic Growth: Evidence for Brazil, Chile and Peru', *Journal of Post Keynesian Economics,* published online. https://doi.org/10.1080/01603477.2016.1136565.

OECD (2015) *'Better Policies' Series—Chile: Policies Priority for Stronger and More Equitable Growth.* Paris: OECD.

OECD (2018) *2018 OECD Economic Survey of Chile, Boosting Productivity and Quality Jobs.* https://www.oecd.org/eco/surveys/Boosting-productivity-and-jobs-Chile-OECD-economic-survey-2018.pdf.

OECD (2020a) *OECD Data, General Government Revenue.* https://data.oecd.org/gga/general-government-revenue.htm.

OECD (2020b) *OECD Revenue Statistics 2019—Chile.* Centre for Tax Policy and Administration. https://www.oecd.org/tax/revenue-statistics-chile.pdf.

Oxhorn, P (1999) 'Is the Country of Corporatism Over? Neoliberalism and the Rise of Neopluralism', in P. Oxhorn and G. Ducatenzeiler, eds, *What Kind of Democracy? What Kind of Market? Latin America in the Age of Neoliberalism.* University Park, PA: Penn State University Press, pp. 195–217.

Panizza, F. E. (1990) 'Accumulation and Consensus in Post-War Uruguay', in Christian Angalde and Carlos Fortin, eds, *The State and Capital Accumulation in Latin America*. London: Macmillan Press, pp. 149–181.

Panizza, Francisco (2000) 'Beyond "Delegative Democracy": "Old Poliitics" and "New Economics" in Latin America', *Journal of Latin American Studies*, 32:3, pp. 737–763.

Pánuco, Humberto and Székeley, Miguel (1996) 'Income Distribution and Poverty in Mexico', in Victor Bulmer-Thomas, ed., *The New Economic Model in Latin America and Its Impact on Income Distribution and Poverty*. London: Macmillan Press, pp. 185–222.

Peluffo, Adriana (2015) 'Foreign Direct Investment, Productivity, Demand for Skilled Labour and Wage Inequality: An Analysis of Uruguay', *The World Economy*, 38:6, pp. 962–983.

Pempel. T. J. (1999) 'The Developmental Regime in a Changing World Economy', in Merdith Woo-Cumings ed., *The Developmental State*. New York; London: Cornell University Press, pp. 137–181.

Pérez, Verónica and Piñeiro-Rodríguez, Rafael (2016) 'Uruguay 2015: The Challenges of the Left Government under Negative Economic Perspectives', *Revista Ciencia Política*, 36:1, pp. 339–363.

Philip, George (1999) 'The Dilemmas of Good Governance: A Latin American Perspective', *Government and Opposition*, 34:2, pp. 226–242.

Richards, Donald G. (1997) 'The Political Economy of the Chilean Miracle', *Latin American Research Review*, 32:1, pp. 139–159.

Robinson, William (1999) 'Latin America in the Age of Inequality: Conforming the New "Utopia"', *International Studies Review*, 1:3, pp. 41–67.

Robinson, William (2000) 'Promoting Capitalist Polyarchy: The Case of Latin America', in M. Cox, G. J. Ikenberry, and T. Inoguchi, eds, *American Democracy Promotion: Impulses, Strategies and Impacts*. Oxford: Oxford University Press, pp. 308–325.

Robinson, William (2002) 'Globalization as a Macro-Structural-Historical Framework of Analysis: The Case of Central America', *New Political Economy*, 7:2, pp. 221–250.

Sheahan, John and Collage, Williams (1997) 'Effects of Liberalization Programs on Poverty and Inequality: Chile, Mexico and Peru', *Latin American Research Review*, 32:3, pp. 7–37.

Silva, Eduardo (1996) 'From Dictatorship to Democracy: The Business-State Nexus in Chile's Economic Transformation, 1975–1994', *Comparative Politics*, 28:3, pp. 299–320.

Starr, Pamela K. (1999) 'Capital Flows, Fixed Exchange Rates and Political Survival: Mexico and Argentina 1994–5', in P. Oxhorn and P. Starr, eds, *Markets and Democracy in Latin America: Conflict or Convergence?* London: Lynne Rienner Publishers, pp. 203–238.

Stuhlberger Wjuniski, Bernardo (2013) 'Education and Development Projects in Brazil (1932–2004): Political Economy Perspective', *Brazilian Journal of Political Economy*, 33:1, pp. 146–165.

Tanski, Janet M. and French, Dan W. (2001) 'Capital Concentration and Market Power in Mexico's Manufacturing Industry: Has Trade Liberalization Made a Difference?', *Journal of Economic Issues*, 35:3, pp. 675–712.

Thirlwall, Anthony P. (1979) 'The Balance of Payments Constraint as an Explanation of International Growth Differences', *Banca Nazionale del Lavoro Quarterly Review*, 32:128, pp. 45–53.

Thomas, Jim (1996) 'The New Economic Model and Labour Markets in Latin America', in Victor Bulmer-Thomas, ed., *The New Economic Model in Latin America and Its Impact on Income Distribution and Poverty*. London: Macmillan Press, pp. 79–102.

Tranjan, Ricardo J. (2012) 'The Political Economy of Participatory Democracy in Brazil: A Case Study of Lages, 1977–1982', *Studies in Political Economy*, 90:1, pp. 137–163.

United Nations (2000) *Global Policy Forum Let's Talk Business*. http://www.globalp olicy.org/reform/2000/1024gc.

United Nations (2001) *The Global Compact: What It Is*. http://www.unglobalcompact. org/un/gc/unweb.nsf/content/whatitis.

United Nations (2002) *Statistics Division*. http://unstats.un.org/unsd/cdb/cdb_dict_ xrxx.asp?def_code=440.

Vernengo, Matías (2007) 'Fiscal Squeeze and Social Policy During the Cardoso Administration (1995–2002)', *Latin American Perspectives*, 156:34, pp. 81–91.

Vernengo, Matías (2008) 'The Political Economy of Monetary Institutions in Brazil: The Limits of the Inflation-Targeting Strategy, 1992–2005', *Review of Political Economy*, 20:1, pp. 95–110.

Vilas, Carlos M. (1997) 'The Ambulancias, Bomberos y Policias: La Politica Social del Neoliberalismo', *Desarrollo Económico*, 36:44, pp. 931–951.

Weber, Heloise (2001) 'The Imposition of a Global Development Architecture: The Example of Microcredit', Centre for the Study of Globalization and Regionalization, Working Paper 77/01.

Weyland, Kurt (1999) 'Economic Policy in Chile's New Democracy', *Journal of Interamerican Studies and World Affairs*, 41:3, pp. 67–96.

Whitehead, Laurence (1996) 'Chronic Fiscal Stress and the Reproduction of Poverty and Inequality in Latin America', in Victor Bulmer-Thomas, ed., *The New Economic Model in Latin America and its Impact on Income Distribution and Poverty*. London: Macmillan Press, pp. 127–143.

Wilkie, James W., Aleman, Eduardo, and Ortega, José Guadalupe (2002) *Statistical Abstract of Latin America*. Los Angeles, CA: Latin American Centre Publications, University of California, 38.

Williamson, John (1990) 'What Washington Means by Policy Reform', in John Williamson ed., *Latin American Adjustment: How Much Has Happened?* Washington, DC: Institute for International Economics, pp. 7–20.

World Bank (1993) *The East Asian Miracle: Economic Growth and Public Policy*. Oxford: Oxford University Press.

World Bank (1997) *World Development Report 1997, The State in a Changing World*. Washington, DC: Oxford University Press.

World Bank (2001a) *World Development Report 2001, Attacking Poverty*. Washington, DC: Oxford University Press.

World Bank (2001b) *World Development Indicators*, CD-ROM. Washington, DC.

World Bank (2020) *World Development Indicators*. Washington, DC. https://datacata log.worldbank.org/dataset/world-development-indicators.

Index

Printed in the United States
By Bookmasters